FROM FEAR TO FAITH

The Spiritual Journey from Anxiety to Trust

Ronald Higdon

FROM FEAR TO FAITH

The Spiritual Journey from Anxiety to Trust

Ronald Higdon

Parson's Porch
Books
Cleveland, TN

Parson's Porch Books

121 Holly Trail, NW
Cleveland, TN 37311

This book was printed in the United States of America.

To order additional copies of this book, contact:
Parson's Porch Books
1-423-475-7308
www.parsonsporch.com

Acknowledgments

It is impossible to thank adequately all of those who contribute to one's journey in life and faith. The years continue to increase my appreciation for the many teachers and professors who gave the best of their subject matter and themselves. I cannot imagine where I would be without them.

So many colleagues and friends have shaped my life and ministry that I could not even begin to list them. They are all a part of the best of what I am; the rest of what I am I assume as my own responsibility.

The congregations where I have attempted to serve as pastor have all made invaluable contributions to my understanding of the Christian faith in a congregational context. This applies to even those with whom I had more than a reasonable amount of conflict, not entirely of their making. And, of course, this is probably where I learned the most.

Perry Bramlett has not only provided ongoing friendship but also a constant supply of quality publications of which I might not otherwise have been aware. His knowledge of the life and work of C.S. Lewis has been shared with countless congregations but that is not the limit of his expertise. For years, he has challenged me to write something like what you now hold in your hands.

And, if there is a dedication, it has to be to my wife, Pat. For over 50 years she has been a source of the kind of encouragement that challenged me to give my best and to give what was most appropriate for the person in the pew. She has an excellent sense of what makes sense.

Table of Contents

Part III: From Fear to Faith in God's Ways

Part IV: From Fear to Faith in Eternal Matters

INTRODUCTION
Biblical Truths in Juxtaposition (Side by Side)

What was anticipated to be "the Christian Century" certainly did not live up to that lofty expectation. To the contrary, it has led us into a new century with more uncertainties, questions, doubts, and anxieties than we ever could have imagined. Whatever happened to "Don't worry, be happy"? Simply put: there are now many more reasons to worry than to be happy (however one defines happiness). Stress, anxiety, apprehension, worry, fear – whatever else you want to add to the list – appear to be major ingredients in a life gone global. Our concerns are no longer local, regional, or even national. The fluttering wings of a butterfly any place in the world can cause a powerful wind of destruction right in our own neighborhood.

In bookstores (the ones that remain), I have noted the progression of large sections of material marked "Self-Help" to "New Age" to "Spirituality." Nancy Malone summarizes my observation: "We have a plethora of popular books on spirituality. But many of them are empty of serious theological consideration, floating like balloons above the religious landscape, unmoored from the beliefs of any tradition at all."[1] My purpose in this book is an attempt to present a "biblically-based spirituality" in the Christian tradition as it relates to the journey from anxiety to trust.

You need to know where I come from when I deal with hermeneutics – the theological term for biblical interpretation. I have always felt it would be helpful if the Bible came with a warning label that read something like this: "Warning! Reading ALL of this book will be dangerous to your spiritual tranquility." Whenever someone tells me that the Bible is the source of their comfort and peace, I always want to say, "True. There is much in the Bible that is an anchor for the soul. But there is much that is disturbing, challenging, and just plain upsetting. What about those parts?" My personal observation has been that often the parts I most wanted to skip over were the parts that provided me with some of the best questions I have ever asked. And, as I have gotten older, my goal has been to ask better and better questions.

Briefly, we need to look at the nature of Holy Scripture. We begin with this observation:

> *Though postmodern people reject rationalism, they have not rejected rationality. People must have some basis for rationality in order to function....The Bible itself has no apparent rationalistic organizational scheme. It does not fit into the neat categories of a book on systematic theology in which topics are pursued in a logical and sequential manner. Yet, the Bible reflects a rational understanding of reality.*[2]

The material in the Bible is not arranged topically,

nor does it come with an index. Study aids heralding "What the Bible says about..." appear to suggest a simplified method to discovering clear and homogenous teachings on just about everything. One often experiences a similar unrecognized temptation when consulting a concordance that references every similar English rendering of a Hebrew or Greek word found throughout Holy Scripture. One of my favorite seminary professors warned against what he termed "kangaroo exegesis": hopping all around in chapters and verses with little or no thought to context or the original intent of the writer. "What the Bible says about..." often strings together unrelated verses whose only similarity is the appearance of a translated key word; the hope of the stringer is to present pearls of biblical wisdom in dazzling coherence.

The often undetected problem with this approach is that one biblical truth is allowed to run roughshod over other biblical truths. In discussing various approaches to apologetics, an author observes: "My sense is that in every case there is a good Christian idea pressed too far, to the point that it is made to run over, or away from, complementary Christian ideas."[3] A better metaphor in attempting to ascertain "what the Bible says" might be a multi-faceted diamond. As one turns the gem to catch reflected light, it is evident that what one sees is but a portion of the totality of the diamond's splendor; each aspect is a part of the whole. The real challenge in biblical interpretation is to find the meaning of a particular verse against the background of the totality of the biblical witness. Failure to do so allows the use of "proof texts" to validate almost anything the reader is seeking to prove. A text may certainly tell us what is true but it may not tell us all that is true about that particular subject. Viewed from another angle, something else may also be true that adds another dimension to the truth discovered in the first text. My favorite "clarity question" is: "That is true. But what else is also true?"

I confess the difficulty of holding many biblical truths in dialectical tension; I also confess the absolute necessity of doing so. When Paul asserts that *now we see in a mirror, dimly...now I known only in part* (I Corinthians 13:12), at least one aspect of what he is admitting is the inability to fit everything neatly together. Knowledge that is partial and fragmentary is not negated because of its incompleteness. Paul is certain that faith, hope, and love abide; he is also certain that love is to have the priority in everything. The love of which he speaks is neither sentimental nor cheap; it is the intentional and persevering *agape* love he defines in I Corinthians 13. With his assertion comes no naïve assumption that the multiple problems in the Corinthian congregation will evaporate in a weekly recitation of an ode to love. There are many other truths that Paul presents to first-century Christian neophytes struggling with difficulties that continue to plague God's assembled saints. To the Corinthians and other gathered communities, Paul presents truth after truth and even the first recipients of his letters found *some things in them hard to understand* (II Peter 3:16). My suspicion is that a failure to hold all of his truths in dialectical tension was no small part of the problem.

The Bible is large in truth but far from simplistic. Mystery, paradox, and ambiguity are writ large throughout the biblical witness. I believe Wayne Booth is correct: "There is pleasure from learning the simple truth, and there is a pleasure from learning that the truth is not simple."[4] The biblical narrative hardly gets under way before the Cain and Abel episode in Genesis 4 presents some weighty challenges. God regards with favor both Abel and his offering; Cain is unacceptable on both counts (although we never get the specifics). To the downcast Cain, God presents the challenge to *do well* and the warning that Cain's anger has the possibility of becoming a lethal weapon. Unsuspecting Abel is lured into the field by his brother and quickly dispatched. Question: where was God? If he knew the danger that Cain's anger portended for Abel, why didn't he post a watching (guardian) angel in the field? Here is a totally innocent victim in a situation of which God is fully aware and does nothing to prevent. The "eye for an eye" folks are probably further outraged that the story ends with God placing a mark on Cain, not as a curse, but in order to protect him. Mystery, paradox, and ambiguity – alive and well even in the book of beginnings.

But not all is mystery, not all is paradox, not all is ambiguity. There are many things in the biblical witness that are clear and direct. The secret in gleaning larger biblical truth is to maintain the tension among the clear, direct, and (hopefully) obvious teachings of specific texts against the background of the entire canon. We, like Paul, may know only in part but we do know some things; we may see in a mirror, dimly, but we do see something. What I will attempt to do in this book is to posit what I believe to be clear teachings from certain biblical texts beside one another in dealing with the theme *From Fear to Faith*. I have not tried to explore subjects, but rather texts. On occasion we may dip into other portions of scripture, but basically we will focus on a particular passage of scripture and seek to ascertain the primary truth or teaching it presents (with a few corollaries thrown in from time to time).

After over fifty years of pastoral ministry, I am convinced that life offers one basic option: fear or faith. The biblical contrast is not between faith and doubt but between faith and fear (faith always understood as trust). This is clearly indicated in Jesus' question to his disciples in Mark 4:40: *"Why are you afraid? Have you no faith?"* The context of this question is an indication of the complexity and difficulty of the faith stance. The disciples are reprimanded for the fear that grips them as they battle a fierce storm in an all but swamped boat. The predicament is compounded further when it is remembered that Jesus is the one who requests the trip to the other side of the lake and that he is in the boat with them – asleep. This is only one of the texts we will explore as we seek to discover ways to move further along the road *From Fear to Faith*.

Our journey is divided into four parts with four chapters in each division: Part I: From Fear to Faith in Our Humanity; Part II: From Fear to Faith in Guidance; Part III: From Fear to Faith in God's Ways; Part IV: From Fear to Faith in Eternal Matters. Following each chapter, there is a brief section titled "Reflections," a place for some additional observations.

As we begin, I can think of no more helpful lines than these from Nancy Malone:

> *From your own life experience, you know that the path we follow in this search doesn't lead us in straight lines directly to our goal, from A to B, or Q, or Z. It is more like the path of a labyrinth, laid out in circuits, with abrupt about-face turns and wide swings, bringing us now nearer to, now farther from the center as we move into it, now nearer to and farther from the outermost rim as we leave it. I see the labyrinth...as a metaphor for our journey through life.*[5]

Unless otherwise noted, scripture references are from the New Revised Standard Version (Division of Christian Education of the National Council of the Churches of Christ in the United States of America, 1989).

[1] Nancy Malone, *Walking a Literary Labyrinth* (New York, Riverhead Books, 2003), 86-87.

[2] Harry Lee Poe, *Christian Witness in a Postmodern World* (Nashville, Abingdon Press, 2001), 130.

[3] John G. Stackhouse, Jr., *Humble Apologetics* , Oxford (Oxford University Press, 2002), 126.

[4] Malone, *Walking a Literary Labyrinth*, 99.

[5] Ibid, 3.

Part I: FROM FEAR TO FAITH IN OUR HUMANITY

Chapter 1: Things Are More Uncertain Than We Thought

MODERN OBSERVATIONS:

This reminds me of the fellow in London after the war (WWII). He's sitting with a parcel wrapped in brown paper in his lap; it's a big, heavy object. The bus conductor comes up to him and says, "What do you have on your lap there?" And the man says, "This is an unexploded bomb. We dug it out of the garden and I'm taking it to the police station." The conductor says, "You don't want to carry that on your lap. Put it under the seat."[1]

Have you ever considered how great an element of paradox there is in human life? The facts of life have a disconcerting way of confounding our careful theories, throwing out our calculations, contradicting our generalizations. Just when we think we have found a formula to fit the facts of life, something unpredictable and eccentric turns up, and makes our neat ship-shape logic look absurd....

You can't hope to get the mystery of it tied up into a neat little formula with no loose ends anywhere....

There will always be awkward, intractable factors turning up, to take our confident theorizing by surprise; always an element of paradox to derange the symmetry of our logic.[2]

THE BIBLICAL TEXT: James 4:13-16:

> *Come now, you who say, "Today or tomorrow we will go to such and such a town and spend a year there, doing business and making money." Yet you do not even know what tomorrow will bring. What is your life? For you are a mist that appears for a while and then vanishes. Instead you ought to say, "If the Lord wishes, we will live and do this or that." As it is, you boast in your arrogance; all such boasting is evil.*

It is difficult for some to believe that the statement found in James 4:14 is actually a verse of scripture. (The Old Testament corollary is found in the wisdom literature of Proverbs 27:1: *Do not boast about tomorrow, for you do not know what a day may bring.)* Those who use the Bible only for comfort and reassurance must skip over this verse (and countless others as well). But it is a verse not to be skipped over. The author begins this section of his letter with an attention grabber so that no one will by-pass this life-jarring reminder. It can be translated in various ways: *Come now....Now listen....Not of word with all who say.* My free translation is: *Now hear this!*

In relation to this text, as well as many others in the pages of scripture, it is wise to keep in mind this observation from Franz Kafka in a letter to his friend Oskar Pollak:

> *Altogether, I think we ought to read only books that bite and sting us. If the book we are reading doesn't shake us awake like a blow on the skull, why bother reading it in the first place? So that it can make us happy, as you put it? Good God, we'd be just as happy if we had no books at all; books that make us happy we could, in a pinch, also write ourselves....A book must be the axe for the frozen sea within us. That is what I believe.*[3]

This brings to mind the warning from the writer of Hebrews: *Indeed, the word of God is living and active, sharper than any two-edged sword, piercing until it divides soul from spirit, joints from marrow; it is able to judge the thoughts and intentions of the heart* (4:12). Here is the verse from the New Living Translation: *For the word of God is full of living power. It is sharper than the sharpest knife, cutting deep into our innermost thoughts and desires. It exposes us for what we really are.*

The totality of the biblical witness (my favorite phrase for good biblical interpretation) provides what I like to call a good dose of "reality therapy." We are challenged to live in a real world that keeps us aware of our need for trust and not new efforts at attempts to control what is beyond our power to control. James 4:14 is one of many reminders that when it comes to the future, attempts to get an advance reading (note the many warnings in the Old Testament about consulting mediums and fortune tellers) are basically non-productive and extremely hazardous to the life of faith.

A modern paraphrase of what we are challenged to hear in our text is: *You don't know the first thing about tomorrow. You're nothing but a wisp of fog, catching a brief bit of sun before disappearing.*[4] In order to deal with our fears, they must be named and confronted head-on. Sometimes renaming helps in the confrontation; this one I call "Truth in Life 101: We can be certain of uncertainty." James insists we acknowledge this all too obvious and easily ignored major aspect of our humanity. James 4:14 underscores uncertainty and instability. I doubt you will find it highlighted in many Bibles, but it should be.

A few years ago in the Metropolitan Diary section of *The New York Times*, a woman told of receiving this notification after asking to reserve a book at the New York Public Library: "The only available copy of the book you reserved is no longer available." The title of the book was "Nothing Can Go Wrong." Many would like to reserve a copy of such a book. Who wants to read: "The Possibilities of Things Going Wrong Are Endless," "Many Less Than Humorous Things Will Happen on the Way to the

Forum," or "Just As I Got All My Ducks in a Row, Hunting Season Began,"? Most of us don't want to read books like these because, if we have lived long enough, we find we could have written them ourselves. But this word of caution: our text is not advocating a cynical or negative approach to life.

Most commentators agree that James is addressing Jewish traders, the great traders of the ancient world, and urging them to consider God in all of their deliberations. In their planning and trading they must be certain they don't leave out God. He also warns against arrogance and boasting. He warns against being so self-assured that one can make plans for an entire year. He warns against the foolish confidence that says, "I am the master of my fate; I am the captain of my soul." [5]

During an interview at a time in his life when he was battling cancer, former NBC news anchor John Chancellor said, "If you want to make God laugh, tell God your plans."[6] I don't understand this to mean you don't make plans; you simply don't presume to hold the future in your hands. You don't succumb to illusions of omnipotence.

The late Carl Sagan kept a framed postcard near his shaving mirror. The message read: "Dear, friend, Just a line to let you know that I am alive and kicking, and going grand." The card was signed by a passenger on the Titanic, and postmarked the day before it went down. Place this along-side the words of Robert F. Goheen, President of

Princeton University, speaking to the graduating class of 1966: "If you feel you have both feet planted on level ground, then the university has failed you." James wants to shake the ground beneath us so that he can get our feet planted on solid, unshakable ground. He wants us to acknowledge the bad news so that he can give us the incredible good news.

He gives the good news like this: *You ought to say, "If the Lord wishes, we will live and do this or that."* "This uncertainty of life is not a cause either for fear or for inaction because of the insecurity of the future. It is a reason for accepting and realizing our complete dependence on God."[7] In the ancient world, it was common practice to include in speaking and in letters the formula "If the gods will...." Even in I Corinthians 4:19, Paul notes, *"I will come to you soon, if the Lord wills."* In earlier generations, many believers placed the initials "D.V." after writing about future appointments. This was an abbreviation for the Latin *Deo volente,* "if the Lord will." James is telling us not only to include God in our planning but to allow God to guide and lead us in our planning.

A basic thesis of Holy Scripture is that God is both willing and able to do this. Psalm 23 includes the phrases: *The Lord is my shepherd...he leads...he guides me.* The nine English words that begin this psalm, *The Lord is my shepherd, I shall not want,* are only four words in Hebrew: *Lord, my-shepherd, not, I-lack.*[8] These four words provide a treasure trove for rich translation possibilities. (We will explore some of these later in chapter 7). The major teaching of the psalm is that just as sheep are not left on their own to find green pastures and still waters, neither are we abandoned to wander around on our own.

An astronomer once said, "If God were to send one of his angels to look for this world amid the glittering hosts of heaven, it would be like sending a child onto the Sahara to pick up one particular grain of sand."[9] There is no doubt about the impossibility of such a task for a child; this as an impossibility for one of God's messengers is another matter. It does, however, raise a legitimate question: Can God know about me and my problems, heartaches, troubles, and dreams lived out on a tiny planet with teeming millions in a universe so vast that it cannot be measured? The testimony of the biblical witness is that the creator God is the covenant God who knows and cares for all of his creation. *(The Lord) heals the brokenhearted, and binds up their wounds. He determines the number of stars; he gives to all of them their names* (Psalm 147:3-4). Psalm 139 gives insight into how detailed is God's perspective: *O Lord, you have searched me and know me. You know when I sit down and when I rise up; you discern my thoughts from far away....Even before a word is on my tongue, O Lord, you know it completely.* The incredulity of this did not escape the psalmist who declares, *"Such knowledge is too wonderful for me; it is so high that I cannot attain it"* (139:6).

In the Genesis story, after the creation of God's good world, the spoiler shows up. He spoiled things then as he spoils them now - by raising the issue of trust. The tempter's question is an attack on God's reliability. "Did God say you couldn't eat of the fruit of any of these trees in the garden?" "Oh, no," comes the response. "With only one exception, we may eat from all of the trees in the garden." "Just as I thought," slithers the circumventor. "God is up to his old tricks again. He's allowing you only the crumbs from his banquet table. That off-limits tree is the best one of all. Once you sink your teeth into a piece of its fruit, you'll take a bite out of real life. If God really wanted what's best for you he wouldn't have imposed these restrictions. He's not to be trusted. Here, take a bite. I guarantee that a whole new world will open up for you." The next words we hear from those whom God made in his image are Adam's words in response to God's, "Where are you?" Adam calls out, "I heard you and I was afraid. So I hid." When you opt out of trust, what you have left is fear. Fear that results in our hiding from God, from one another, and from ourselves. The purpose of the biblical story is to bring about a reversal of what happened in Eden, to bring us from fear to relational trust.

I have never forgotten the line from a song I heard many years ago: "I know not what the future holds, but I know who holds the future." This idea is majestically stated in Psalm 90:1-2: *Lord, you have been our dwelling place in all generations. Before the mountains were brought forth, or ever you had formed the earth and the world, from everlasting to everlasting you are God.* We are called to trust the One who holds yesterday, today, and tomorrow in his hands. A pivotal message from Jesus was, "Trust in God; trust also in me. Trust the God who knows and cares for you personally. Why, even the very hairs of your head are all counted" (John 14:1; Matthew 10:30). The God upon whom James is calling us to depend is the God who has made himself known to us most clearly in Jesus Christ. When you say, "If the Lord wills...," it is the Lord who knows all about you, loves you incredibly, and wants you to become more than even you in your wildest dreams have ever imagined.

In verse 17 James gives his piece of advice for living with the uncertainty and brevity of life. Most commentators believe the verse is a proverb current in the day; some have speculated that it could be a saying of Jesus.[10] *Anyone, then, who knows the right thing to do and fails to do it, commits sin.* I maintain that it is almost impossible to pray, "Lord, show me something I ought to be doing right now," and come from prayer without an answer, an answer we usually already know. James' call to us is the title of a book from some years ago: "Do It! Do It! Do It!" The call is for action, action, action. Today. Right now.

A university professor often assigned a paper in

which students were asked the question, "If you had only five days to live, how would you spend those five days? And with whom?" The responses varied but the note the professor attached to each paper was the same: "Why don't you do these things NOW?" This is exactly what James says to each of us. Uncertain times have always been the order of the day. Our uncertainty does not have to be an added ingredient. We can pray and live the following prayer:

> *O God, we thank you for this day. Open our eyes that we may let none of its wonders pass unseen. Give us a courageous positive interest in everything that happens around us. Help us to lay hold upon every opportunity to be of use this day, and then take from our hearts all vain regrets and all empty dreams of the future that we may follow him who went about day by day doing the good of that day, Jesus Christ, our Lord. Amen. (Source unknown).*

Reflections

It has already been obvious to the reader that I am presenting material as I understand it. When someone offers "their take" on a particular issue, I will often ask, "And your point of view is based on what?" In *Life Is Mostly Edges*, Calvin Miller writes: "John and Sophie taught me that it is not enough to believe in something sincerely. It is also important to be informed."[11] I have tried to base my "understanding" of things on my years of continuing formal education, constant reading, learning through dialogue, and prayerful reliance on the guidance of the Spirit as I explore biblical texts. This, however, in no way means that I consider what I have to say the final word or even the flawless word on anything. I simply want you to know that what I have written is not based on what I happen to feel passionately about at the moment.

This is why I have a suggestion as you continue reading. When you come to a statement with which you strongly agree, pencil an "A" in the margin. When you read something with which you strongly disagree, put a "D" beside it. When you read anything you feel needs clarification, mark that place with a "?". These will be the subjects for your own reflections. One of my Dad's favorite responses to a request from any of his children was, "Let me mull that over." (The Bible calls it "pondering.") In a culture with "information overload" and very little (if any) time for reflection, I have found it necessary to be intentional about pauses that create the space for true learning experiences. Also, I have long ago accepted that "Fear is a question." Whenever I read something that brings about a strong emotion or creates anxiety, I ask myself, "What am I afraid of?"

In this chapter, I used the phrase "the totality of the biblical witness." I cannot stress too much the necessity for being constantly aware of the BIG picture and viewing every text in this larger context. Along with this comes my very strong conviction that the key to understanding God's revelation is to begin with the highest and clearest revelation in Jesus Christ. Hebrews 1:1-3 insists that Jesus is the *reflection of God's glory and the exact imprint of God's very being.* In Jesus we have the disclosure of what God had in mind all the time for an understanding of what he is about in this world. *"Whoever has seen me has seen the Father"* (John 14:9) is Jesus' corrective for his time and all time about conjectures concerning the nature and purposes of God. My rules of thumb may shock you: If I can't put the words in the mouth of Jesus, I don't put them in the mouth of God. If I can't picture Jesus doing it, I don't picture God doing it.

There is the story about the young girl reading through the entire Bible with her mother and finally asking, "As God got older, did he get better?" Another way of asking that question is: "Is God as good as Jesus?" The Bible declares in no uncertain terms that in Jesus Christ we see what God has always been like. We see the One who is the same from everlasting to everlasting. (Many may want to put a question mark in the margin here. You may even want to put a D!) I cannot make "sense" out of the biblical revelation unless I view all the scriptures through the lenses of God's final Word – the Living Word. John 1:14: *And the Word became flesh and lived among us, and we have seen his glory, the glory as of the Father's only son, full of grace and truth.* John 14:6: *Jesus said, "I am the way, and the TRUTH, and the life."* What does it mean for truth to be a person? The least it means is that you don't believe a proposition, you trust a person. (That statement during a Bible study always creates some genuine excitement.)

This does not mean that in Jesus we have come to know everything about God. In Jesus, we have come to know everything we need to know about God. What the

Lord said to Isaiah, he says to us (55:9): ... *my ways higher than your ways and my thoughts are than your thoughts.* Paul "updates" the idea in Romans 11:33: *O the depth of the riches and wisdom and knowledge of God! How unsearchable are his judgments and how inscrutable his ways!*

[1]Anthony deMello, *Awareness* (New York, Image Books, 1992), 41-42.

[2]James S. Stewart, *The Strong Name* (New York, Charles Scribner's Sons, 1941), 116-117.

[3]Malone, *Walking a Literary Labyrinth*, 117-118.

[4]Eugene H. Peterson, *The Message* (Colorado Springs, Navipress, 2002), 2207.

[5]*The Broadman Bible Commentary*, Volume 12 (Nashville, Broadman Press, 1972), 130.

[6]*Homiletics*, Volume 8, Number 3, July-September 1996, 22.

[7]William Barclay, *The Letters of James and Peter* (Philadelphia, Westminster Press, 1960), 134.

[8]James L. Kugel, *The Great Poems of the Bible* (New York, The Free Press, 1999), 193.

[9]Leslie D. Weatherhead, *That Immortal Sea* (New York, Abingdon Press, 1953), 128.

[10]Peter Davids, *New International Greek Testament Commentary, Commentary on James* (Grand Rapids, Wm. B. Eerdmans Publishing Co.), 174.

[11]Calvin Miller, *Life Is Mostly Edges* (Nashville, Thomas Nelson, 2008), 155.

Chapter 2: Will God Put a Hedge Around Those Who Are His?

MODERN OBSERVATIONS:

A pious elderly woman, after the Second World War, remarked: "God was very good to us. We prayed and prayed, so all the bombs fell on the other side of town."[1]

Jesus promised his disciples three things: that they would be completely fearless, absurdly happy, and in constant trouble. F. R. Maltby.

One of the biggest lies within the body of Christ claims that once we accept Christ, our lives will be free from problems.[2]

Every day I put hope on the line. I don't know one thing about the future. I don't know what the next hour will hold. There may be sickness, personal or world catastrophe. Before this day is over I may have to deal with death, pain, loss, rejection. I don't know what the future holds for me, for those whom I love, for my nation, for this world. Still, despite my ignorance and surrounded by tinny optimists and cowardly pessimists, I say that God will accomplish his will and cheerfully persist in living in the hope that nothing will separate me from Christ's love.[3]

THE BIBLICAL TEXT: Job 1:6-11:

> *The day came when the members of the court of heaven took their places in the presence of the Lord, and the Adversary, Satan, was among them. The Lord asked him where he had been. "Ranging over the earth," said the Adversary, "from end to end." The Lord asked him, "Have you considered my servant Job? You will find no one like him on earth, a man of blameless and upright life, who fears God and sets his face against wrongdoing."*

"Has not Job good reason to be godfearing?" answered the Adversary. "Have you not hedged him round on every side with your protection, him and his family and all his possessions? Whatever he does you bless, and everywhere his herds have increased beyond measure. But stretch out your hand and touch all that he has, and see if he will not curse you to your face."[4]

Anyone who is not perplexed by the book of Job must have skipped over the first two chapters. The book begins with a mystifying prologue that raises some serious questions about the life of faith. Does it pay to be good, but not too good? (Job gets noticed in the heavenly council due to his extraordinary righteousness. If these are regular meetings, you certainly hope your name never comes up!) Is God into game-playing with our lives? (Job is never told about the contest that lies behind the calamities in his life.) Is God willing to allow our children to be sacrificed to prove a point? (Job loses his property and his children in quick succession.) Does God allow Satan to bring him reports from the field? (Surely more reliable and far less adversarial messengers are in readiness.) Does God just stand by and let anything happen to us? (Short of killing Job, God grants Satan full reign: *The Lord said to Satan, "Very well, all that he has is in your power...."* Job 1:12.)

When, after thirty-seven chapters, God finally responds to Job's demands for an audience, he turns the tables by becoming the cross-examiner: *Then the Lord answered Job out of the storm. He said, "Brace yourself like a man; I will question you, and you will answer me"* (Job 38:1, 3). Job is a book filled with questions (and questioners): God questions Satan, Satan questions God, Job's three friends (Eliphaz, Bildad, and Zophar) question Job, Job questions his three friends, Job insists he wants to question God (23:5), and, finally, God questions Job. And the book of Job questions all of us.

Too often it is assumed that Job is a biblical treatise dealing with the issue of why the righteous suffer. If this is its intent, it fails miserably. The major question that the book of Job addresses is plainly stated in 1:9-10: *Has not Job good reasons to be godfearing? Have you not hedged him round on every side with your protection?* Or as it is phrased in this chapter title: Does God put a hedge around those who are his? Translations like the King James do not reflect that only the first two chapters, a few verses in chapter 32, and two-thirds of chapter 42, are prose. Attempting to interpret a book that is over 90% poetry mandates a different approach than one would use when reading Exodus. Some matters are so large that only the language of poetry will suffice; some things are better explored through singing and praying (as in the Psalms); some matters are so inexplicable that the only "resolution" is a doxology (as in Romans 11:33-36, Paul's conclusion to his agony over Israel's rejection of Jesus as the Messiah).

A number of commentators contend that, like so many literary classics, Job is known and discussed, but rarely read. "It is in reading the book that one makes some revelatory discoveries. One of the heavenly beings bringing reports to God is called Satan. In the Hebrew text you discover that the definite article 'the' precedes the word Satan: 'the Satan.' This indicates a title and means 'the accuser' or 'the adversary.'"[5] It has been suggested that the question *"Where have you come from?"* is another way of asking, *"Have you been doing your job?"* The Satan's reply offers no specifics other than an affirmative answer to the inquiry. It is God who introduces Job into the discussion. *"Have you considered my servant Job?"* Tagging Job as "my servant" puts him in the category with the likes of Abraham and Moses. God boasts that there is no one else on earth as blameless and upright as Job .

Then The Satan throws a couple of real zingers at God. He declares, "Of course, Job is good! It pays him to be good! He serves you and you unload tons of benefits on him. Plus, you're in the protection racket. You've thrown a hedge around him to protect him. No wonder he's so good! You just let some bad things happen to him and you'll see how fast he'll forsake you and all your ways." God accepts the challenge and the contest begins with neither Job nor any of his friends ever becoming aware of the background for all the calamitous events that darken the life of a person extraordinary in goodness.

If taken literally, the book of Job offers an array of theological minefields. If we listen to its central message, it speaks with singular clarity. God is not in the hedge business. Being good does not protect us from the hazards of life that come to all people. Sometimes it rains on your parade or your ballgame, not because of anything you have done, but simply because we live in a world where sometimes it rains. And sometimes it pours! Rabbi Harold Kushner has said, "Expecting the world to treat you fairly because you are a good person is like expecting the bull not to charge you because you are a vegetarian."

There are many hazards on the road of life and they are there for everyone. I vividly remember a young man who lived with his family in the Shenandoah Valley of Virginia. He was an exceptional youth from an exceptional family whose life at eighteen was full of promise; he was in every respect the ideal son who was the pride of his family. Allen (not his real name) bought a new FM stereo radio for his car and, with a friend, drove the five miles to the Blue Ridge Parkway to find out how many stations could be picked up from this excellent reception site. Night came and they did not return. At three o'clock in the morning the car was found down a mountain side, smashed against a tree. Allen's friend was injured, but survived. Allen was pronounced dead on the scene.

As I sat with the family, the father's cry was, "Why? Why? Why?" The facts were that the curve on the Blue Ridge Parkway where the car went off the road was covered with gravel. Perhaps the gravel had been spilled from a truck; no one knew how it got there. Allen was probably driving a little too fast and the tires couldn't maintain traction when they hit the gravel. God didn't send an angel to brush the gravel off the road. The laws of physics were not suspended. Allen's life was snuffed out in an instant. The father kept repeating the phrase, "What a waste!" And he was right. I had no answer for the question "Why?" I have no answer now. I simply joined with the family as together we wept.

What I do know is that Job's three friends are all wrong. God says they are wrong. He speaks to Eliphaz: *"My wrath is kindled against you and your two friends; for you have not spoken of me what is right, as my servant Job has"* (42:7). The three friends contend that good things happen to good people and bad things happen to bad people. They keep insisting that Job's troubles must be the consequence of sin in his life. Job can't shout them down but God finally does: "No! I simply did not put a protective hedge around Job. He's mine and I love him, but there is no hedge." This is one of those places of thickly textured biblical complexity:

> *We should be troubled by the fact that the typical mass market self-help book, consumed by many college-educated readers, is accessible to anyone with a decent eight-grade education. We should worry about the willingness of so many to believe that the answers to existential questions can be encapsulated in the portentous pronouncements of bumper-sticker books. Only people who die very young learn all they really need to know in kindergarten.6*

So many of these mass market self-help books are read by well-meaning people of faith who are desperately trying to find something to hang onto in these chaotic times. Checking reality at the door, however, is not the way to begin. It is the old "good news, bad news" scenario. Most of the bumper-stick books ignore the reality of what can only be called evil and also ignore the clear biblical teachings about what we can expect in this world. I don't know how you can explain away II Timothy 3:10-12: *Now you have observed my teaching, my conduct, my aim in life, my faith, my patience, my love, my steadfastness, my persecutions and suffering the things that happened to me in Antioch, Iconium, and Lystra. What persecutions I endured! Yet the Lord rescued me from all of them. Indeed, all who want to live a godly life in Christ Jesus will be persecuted.*

The book of Job offers a post-graduate course in religion and life. It is not for the faint-hearted or the simple-minded. It is not a bumper-sticker book. Bumper-stickers (or what I like to call "auto exhaust wisdom") are usually hazardous to one's theological health. The Bible never deals with the most challenging question for people of faith: "Why does a good all-powerful God permit evil?" Biblically, evil is accepted as a fact in the world, the world God has made. In Romans 8:18-25, Paul briefly discusses a theological concept that comes right in the middle of his great chapter on God's intimate involvement with our lives in this world and the assurance of his love and commitment to us in spite of anything that may come our way: *hardship, distress, persecution, famine, nakedness, peril, or sword* (8:35). His thesis is that we are living in a world that is not yet fully redeemed: *We know that the whole creation has been groaning in labor pains until now* (8:22). Things are not yet what God intends. Full redemption, for us and for the entire creation, awaits that time when there is *a new heaven and a new earth (and) death and mourning and crying and pain will be no more* (Revelation 21). Not until then will redemption have reached its consummation. During this "interim time" I am reminded of the old saw: "Meanwhile, back at the ranch...."

Proof texts to the contrary, the central teaching of scripture is that God does not send suffering and pain and trouble in life, even though in the final analysis he has to permit it. It is the adversary in Job who is the source of all the evil that befalls Job. James 1:17 is one of the biblical mountaintops: *Every generous act of giving, with every perfect gift, is from above, coming down from the Father of lights, with whom there is no variation or shadow due to change.* God is consistent in goodness, grace, mercy, and love.

Trouble often comes as a result of our foibles, mistakes, and foolish choices, but all too often it comes because we are living in a world filled with trouble of all kinds. It is a world full of paradox, mystery, and ambiguity. Instead of reducing some of the perplexities in life, when God begins speaking in Job 38 he simply launches into an Audubon Society tour and a National Geographic lecture. Rather than addressing Job's troubles, God talks about the sunrise, snow, thunderstorms, a lioness, mountain goats, wild donkeys, the ostrich, the horse, the hawk, the eagle, and the crocodile. God enlarges the mysteries of Job's world until Job confesses: *"I have uttered what I did not understand, things too wonderful for me, which I did not know"* (42:3).

If God does not put a hedge around those who are his, is there anything he does for us? I recall the story of a father talking to the young man who had been dating his daughter. With a smile, he proudly announces, "Son, whoever marries my daughter will get a prize." With wide-eyed wonder, the young man asks, "Really? What is it?" While we still have an eye for the obvious, I ask, "What is the prize in biblical faith?" The Satan's charge in the prologue is that Job is faithful because of the benefits he receives from God; these benefits are defined exclusively as "the good things in life." The real benefit of Job's religion, the real benefit of his faith, is God.

The ending of the book of Job assures us that God never abandons Job. God may not put a hedge around Job but God put himself around Job. God is with Job at the beginning of the book; God is with Job at the end of the book. The doubling of Job's fortune is secondary to the strong statements about Job's relationship with God. In response to Job's prayers for them, God pledges not to deal with Eliphaz, Bildad, and Zophar according to their folly. The Lord blesses Job and Job dies *old and full of years* (42:7). These are the very same words used of Abraham in Genesis 25:8. As the prayers of Abraham save Lot from the destruction of Sodom, so the prayers of Job spare his three friends the consequences of their wordy mischief. Similarity in epitaphs and intercessory prayers indicate a similarity in relationship to God, a relationship that is the true prize in the life of faith. And better than a hedge any day.

Reflections

Some lines provide graphic descriptions that we don't soon forget: "Our shoeless tour on a roadway of shattered glass was over. Today we both can say it is easier to find Christ in our brokenness than in our meager achievements."[7] This was not the first time the writer of those sentences had taken such a "tour." Even after explaining the benefit of such an experience, we still wonder why any of God's children are forced to endure such painful experiences. We will explore this question further in the next chapter, but for now we have to conclude that God does not put a protective hedge around those who are his. If there is shattered glass on our roadway of life and we are shoeless, well....

I have heard many testimonies from those who did believe that God was in the hedge business, but I still don't believe it. I've lived too long. I've seen too much. We face what everyone in the world faces living in an unfinished world (more about that later). God did not put a hedge even around his own son: Hebrews 4:15: *...we do not have a high priest who is unable to sympathize with our weaknesses, but we have one who in EVERY respect has been tested as we are, yet without sin.*

If there is a great lesson from the book of Job, it is not the one that is sometimes echoed in the phrase "the patience of Job." This saying came as a result of the King James mistranslation of James 5:11: *Ye have heard of the patience of Job.* Neither James nor anyone else who has ever read the book of Job has heard of that! Job is far from patient (see 12:2; 13:3-4; 16:2). The Greek word *hypomone* does not mean patience but perseverance in difficult circumstances. I *have* heard of the perseverance of Job! This we do see in Job: 1:21-22; 2:10; 13:15; 19:25-27. The great lesson from the book has to do with tenacity, the ability to "hang in there." This is really a step above a passive endurance. There is nothing passive about the perseverance of Job.

Early in my pastoral ministry, I found a quote from an unknown source that became one of our pieces of "refrigerator wisdom." It read: "I'm going to quit; but not today."

At the fall opening convocation at a large university, the speaker challenged the students with these words:

Instead of preparing you for "success" we should be

preparing you to cope with failure when things don't turn out right – whether it is your marriage, your job, your children, or your nation. We should all along have been inculcating in you...capacities for endurance. Instead of breeding eagles we should have been breeding camels who will make it across the desert because they have what they require on the inside and will not quit. Camels have staying power; camels are what we want.[8]

[1] Anthony deMello, *Taking Flight* (New York, Image Books, 1990), 28.

[2] Stephen Arterburn, *The God of Second Chances* (Nashville, Thomas Nelson Publishers, 2002), 21.

[3] Eugene H. Peterson, *A Long Obedience in the Same Direction* (Downers Grove, Il., Inter-Varsity Press, 1980), 72.

[4] *The Revised English Bible* (Oxford, Oxford University Press, 1989), 431.

[5] John C. L. Gibson, *Job* (Philadelphia, Westminster Press, 1985), 11.

[6] Wendy Kaminer, *I'm Dysfunctional, You're Dysfunctional* (Reading, Massachusetts, Addison-Wesley Publishing Company, 1992), 7.

[7] Calvin Miller, *Life Is Mostly Edges*, 248.

[8] Peter Gomes, *Strength for the Journey* (New York, HarperOne, 2003), 302.

Chapter 3: Isn't There a Logical Explanation for the Bad Things in Life?

MODERN OBSERVATIONS:

...in no time the four of us were remarking on the social and economic and political aspects of that phenomenon – lest an assertively unqualified psychology be allowed to strip a particular human scene of its thickly textured complexity.[1]

It is not so much the suffering as the senselessness of it that is unendurable. Friedrich Nietzsche.

I have a book on my shelf, *Theories of Illness*, that surveys 139 tribal groups from around the world; all but four of them perceive illness as a sign of God's (or the gods') disapproval.[2]

THE BIBLICAL TEXT: John 9:1-7:

> *As he walked along, he saw a man blind from birth. His disciples asked him, "Rabbi, who sinned, this man or his parents that he was born blind?" Jesus answered, "Neither this man nor his parents sinned; he was born blind so that God's works might be revealed in him. We must work the works of him who sent me while it is day; night is coming when no one can work. As long as I am in the world, I am the light of the world." When he had said this, he spat on the ground and made mud with the saliva and spread the mud on the man's eyes saying to him, "Go, wash in the pool of Siloam" (which means Sent). Then he went and washed and came back able to see.*

Even though Jesus plainly teaches that it is incorrect, the assumption behind the question put to Jesus by his disciples is one many continue to make. In the course of a teaching-walk with their Rabbi, the band of learners comes upon a familiar sight, the regular begging station of a man who has been blind since birth. As he sits there with closed eyes and open hand, instead of crossing his palm with a coin, the disciples ask a question revealing their philosophy of how life works: *"Who sinned, this man or his parents that he was born blind?"*

The way they figure life works and the assumption in back of their question is simple: when you see bad things in life you know that somebody is to blame. The tragedy of this man's blindness is the result of wrongdoing by somebody; the disciples simply want Jesus to tag the guilty party. If they had known about the survey of 139 tribal groups in which all but four perceived illness as a sign of God's (or the gods') disapproval, they would have added their "amen" to the 135 groups.

Two little boys meet and the following conversation ensues: "How old are you?" "I'm five. How old are you?" "I don't know." "You don't know how old you are?" "Nope." "Do girls bother you?" "Nope." "You're four."

All you have to do is live long enough and some things will start to bother you. Some things will begin to loom large with mystery. One of the most disturbing of these bothering things is the apparent randomness of so much suffering. We soon discover that not only do bad things happen to good people, terrible things happen to wonderful people. The question from the disciples is only an effort to put a little order, reason, and logic into things that threaten to scare the daylights out of us. If bad/tragic things can happen to anybody, anywhere, anytime, what kind of a world is this? In an ordered universe, a causation factor must be a foregone conclusion. When somebody sins, breaks God's law, then according to the thinking of the disciples, it is "sock it to me time" and God does the socking.

William Barclay (1907-1978) is widely known for his authorship of a New Testament commentary series. In one of his weekly radio broadcasts he talked about the tragic boating accident in which his daughter and soon to be son-in-law were drowned. A listener sent an anonymous letter that stated: "Dear Dr. Barclay, I now know why God killed your daughter; it was to save her from being corrupted by your heresies." Barclay made this response: "If I had had that writer's address, I would have written back, not in anger – the inevitable blaze of anger was over in a flash – but in pity, and I would have said to him, as John Wesley said to someone: 'Your God is my devil.' The day my daughter was lost at sea there was sorrow in the heart of God."[3]

When you are seeking an explanation for the bad things in life, if you are not careful, you can easily make God into a devil. What kind of a God would strike down two young people because a father said something somebody considered heresy? What kind of a God would bring a sightless baby into the world in order to get even with parents who had failed somewhere in faithful living? Consequences and deeds can often be connected; all too often, there appears to be no correlation. The undeserving are all too often recipients of pain, injustice, and calamity. There are too many tragedies that are totally out of line with anyone's misbehavior. There is simply too much excessive suffering in the world to fit the consequential equation theory.

I remember doing a Bible study week many years ago at a church in northern Virginia. On the last night of the study, a man, his wife, and son came to the supper and stayed for the session. I'll tell you about him: he was diabetic, blind, and had lost 50% of his hearing. He started learning Braille and lost the feeling of touch in his fingers. He was only 35 years old and his son was 5. During the time for discussion at the end of the study, he told us, "I have prayed to get well. I don't think I will. So many things are wrong. I have prayed for strength and for my family not to suffer as I have suffered." By the time he got through, there wasn't a dry eye in the room and the reminder of a world large with mystery, paradox, and ambiguity.

I Corinthians 13 is certainly for many a favorite chapter in the Bible. In that great chapter on love (and faith and hope), Paul has a phrase whose punch easily can be missed. He says, *For now we see in a mirror, dimly....*It comes as a shock to some to discover that the usual translation "dimly" in the Greek literally means "in a riddle." Some translate the word as "enigma." In talking about his faith, Paul dares to use such words as riddle and enigma. Sometimes we see in a mirror extremely dimly!

Some things, however, we ought to be able to see. How can anyone miss Jesus' answer to the question, *"Who sinned, this man or his parents, that he was born blind?"* His answer is, *"Neither."* (Based on the account in Genesis 25:22 of the yet to be born Jacob and Esau struggling together, many concluded it was possible to sin before one was born.) With a single word, Jesus refutes the almost universally accepted principle of his day that all suffering reflects sin. The book of Job ought to have settled that. Psalm 103:3 ought to settle that: *If you, O Lord, should mark iniquities, Lord, who could stand?* The unvoiced answer is, "Nobody!" It is theologically untenable to assert that God has decided to zap it to some folks and not to others. Unfortunately, those who maintain this position are convinced they know which sins are zap-worthy: yours and not theirs. A possible shocking corollary to such a position is that if people deserve suffering, why should we have compassion on them or attempt to do anything to alleviate their pain?

The answer to the question, "What have I done to deserve this?" is more often than not: "You just showed up!" In a Kudzu comic strip, Doug Marlette drafts a conversation between Kudzu and Rev. Will B. Dunn. Kudzu asks, "Tell me, preacher, Why me?" He puts his head down, pounds his fist on a wooden railing and repeats, "Why me? Why me? Why me?" The preacher responds, "Why not?" Rev. Will B. Dunn is much closer to biblical truth than are many who attempt to give a logical explanation for the bad things in life.

Instead of attempting an explanation as to why this man was born blind, Jesus prescribes a course of action: *He was born blind so that God's works might be revealed in him.* Meaning: *I will use his blindness as an opportunity to demonstrate the grace and goodness of God.* In Jesus' teaching ministry, I do not discover any lengthy dissertations on the problem of evil and suffering in the world. In the Gospel of Mark we are told that Jesus goes about doing good (3:4). His is a plan of action in the midst of much that is beyond explanation. In his use of a personal pronoun I find a mountain of instruction: *"WE must work the works of him who sent me while it is day...."* We are not called to explanation, but to action.

With the writer's permission, I give you a letter I have used in several sermons because it is about real people in a real world sharing real faith:

Precious Friends:

There was a time when I thought that if God heard/loved me, he wouldn't let certain things happen to me or mine. Then, through reading, I was reminded that he did not single out his Son/himself for favored treatment, but let the price of an imperfect world be paid by himself. And thus it remains: his "heirs" continue to pay the price of living in an imperfect world. No one is spared indefinitely, with the price extracted in various ways.

My temporal self weeps over your new news and the prospect of your forthcoming battle against cancer. I am never cavalier about human hurt because I have been where there was for a time no light and remember the anguish. However, I know that regardless of the outcome, the desire of God's heart is to provide for his children and to show himself to you through his earthly "lovers" – family and friends (wondrous gifts!). This he will do in abundance, filling each of us and you with his Spirit so that there can be no doubt that his promise is true: I will be with you; I will not fail you or forsake you (Joshua 1:5). And together we shall live one day at a time, giving thanks for all that remains good in our lives, secure in the knowledge that regardless of outward circumstances, God is love.

All I can do now is to take hold of your hand and walk with you to wherever it is we are going, praying all the while that God's peace that passes all understanding undergirds the human journey and teaches us new things about love for one another and his love for us.

You will never be out of our thoughts and prayers. We love you. P.S. The Holy Spirit gave to me the above message for you. Although I know in my spirit its truth, I need to tell you that I have kept a copy for myself as I often need to remind myself of what I know. There are times when I'd just like to scream and swear – and do. If you'd ever like to join me in one of these fits, just call and I'll run right over! In fact, I offer curb service for any purpose. But fit-pitching is a specialty.

Hugs, _____(Signed).

I marked this line in a book dealing with suffering and evil: "When life comes to pieces, no amount of explanation will fill the void."[4] "Why?" is the unproductive, defeating approach to suffering. "What?" can be a positive, helpful, active discovery of something to be done while looking the problem squarely in the face. Even if Jesus had provided a profound theory to the problem of suffering, what good would it have done the blind man? His blindness would have remained. "The disciples approached tragedy in search of someone to blame, whereas Jesus was concerned with what he could change."[5]

In this situation, Jesus says, *"As long as I am in the world, I am the light of the world."* To all of his disciples in whatever situation, he says, *"You are the light of the world"* (Matthew 5:14). In the darkness of his world, Jesus brings the light of God's grace, mercy, love, hope, forgiveness, and healing. He doesn't waste time wringing his hands or expending energy cursing the darkness. He is about his Father's business of bringing light to valleys as dark as death itself (Psalm 23:4). We are called to live in our world the way Jesus lived in his world. We are to be short on explanation and long on action.

Reflections

This, of course, is THE question that won't go away: How can a truly good and all powerful God permit all the bad things that are so much a part of life? The natural conclusion is: either God is not all good or he is not all powerful. Some have concluded that God is not all powerful; there are some things he cannot do. This is the conclusion of Rabbi Harold Kushner in his book *When Bad Things Happen to Good People.* Chapter seven is titled "God

Can't Do Everything, But He Can Do Some Important Things." This book was precipitated by the diagnosis of his son at age three with progeria, "rapid aging." I cannot imagine the pain involved in caring for this son until his death at fourteen.

After thirty years, I still find it to be an excellent book because Kushner does not attempt to defend or explain God. He writes:

> *I am not a formally trained philosopher. I am fundamentally, a religious man who has been hurt by life and I wanted to write a book that could be given to the person who has been hurt by life – by death, by illness or injury, by rejection or disappointment – and who knows in his heart that if there is justice in the world, he deserved better.*[6]

Many people have found comfort and encouragement from this honest treatment of faith's greatest dilemma. Unfortunately, during their dark days, some offered the Kushners all the classic explanations you have heard – explanations that only deepen the pain and confusion. These explanations, I believe, were offered by well-meaning people who were terrified to think that there might not be a "logical" explanation for the bad things in life.

As difficult as it is to do, I prefer to maintain what I believe to be the biblical teaching: God is good and he is all powerful (omnipotent). God does not expect a negative answer to the question he asks: *Is anything too hard for the Lord?* (Genesis 18:14; *New International Version).* If this is our thesis, then we have to ask, why doesn't God do something about the awful things in life? Why is there evil? I am unwilling to let go of either end of this paradox. I am unwilling to let go of the mystery and ambiguity I find in life and faith. That means my calling is to stand with those who question "Why?" and find no answer except in the assurance of God's presence and the support and presence of God's people.

[1] Robert Coles, *Harvard Diary II* (New York, Crossroad Publishing, 1997), 51.

[2] Philip Yancey, *Where is God When It Hurts?* (Grand Rapids Zondervan, 1990), 77.

[3] William Barclay, *Testament of Faith* (London, Mowbrays, 1975), 45-46.

[4] R. Kirby Godsey, *When We Talk About God* (Macon, Smyth & Helwys, 1996), 99.

[5] *The Broadman Bible Commentary*, Volume 9 (Nashville, Broadman Press, 1970), 298.

[6] Harold S. Kushner, *When Bad Things Happen To Good People* (New York, Schocken Books, 1981), 5.

Chapter 4: How Do You Have Faith
When the Boat is Sinking?

MODERN OBSERVATIONS:
"So this was your first flight. Were you scared?"
"Well, to tell the truth, I didn't dare put my full weight down on the seat."[1]

Most of these Old Testament characters show up in the honor roll of Hebrews 11, a chapter some have labeled "The Faith Hall of Fame." I prefer to call that chapter, "Survivors of the Fog," for many of the heroes listed have one common experience: a dread time of testing like Job's, a time when the fog descends and everything goes blank. Torture, jeers, floggings, chains, stoning, sawings in two – Hebrews records in grim detail the trials that may befall faith-full people.

Saints become saints by somehow hanging on to the stubborn conviction that things are not as they appear, and that the unseen world is as solid and trustworthy as the visible world around them. God deserves trust, even when it looks like the world is caving in.[2]

THE BIBLICAL TEXT: Luke 8:22-25:

> One day, Jesus said to his disciples, "Let's cross over to the other side of the lake." So they got into a boat and started out. On the way across, Jesus lay down for a nap, and while he was sleeping the wind began to rise. A fierce storm developed that threatened to swamp them, and they were in real danger. The disciples woke him up, shouting, "Master, Master, we're going to drown!" So Jesus rebuked the wind and the raging waves. The storm stopped and all was calm! Then he asked them, "Where is your faith?" And they were filled with awe and amazement. They said to one another, "Who is this man, that even the winds and waves obey him?"[3]

Many are perplexed when they read this episode from Luke's gospel and their confusion has nothing to do with the calming of the storm. They are bewildered because of Jesus' seeming attitude of indifference. Everywhere else Jesus is solidly in touch with reality; everywhere else he is sympathetic and supportive of people in difficulty. Here Jesus appears to be totally insensitive to his disciples. He asks them what appears to be a ludicrous question, *"Where is your faith?"* I'll tell you where it was; it got drenched, it got waterlogged.

If you've never witnessed a sudden squall on Lake Galilee, you have no idea how sudden, severe, and dangerous such storms can be. Luke tells us that *the wind began to rise (and) a fierce storm developed that threatened to swamp* the small boat containing Jesus and his disciples. An expanded translation provides a more dramatic picture: *...there came down a whirlwind on the lake, breaking forth out of black thunderclouds in furious gusts, with floods of rain, throwing everything topsy-turvy, and (the boat was) filling with water....*[4] That puts Jesus' question, *"Where is your faith?"*, in proper perspective. It gives us a question most of us hope we will never have to address: "How do you have faith when the boat is sinking?"

If the disciples had not been tongue-tied with stupefaction, I can think of a probable answer they might have given to Jesus' question: "To tell you the truth, we didn't expect a storm like this because, after all, you're the one who told us to cross over to the other side of the lake." Many believe that when life is full of trouble and difficulty it is a sure sign they are living outside "the will of God." Here the disciples strictly obey a direct command from their Lord and find themselves in the middle of such a fierce storm that they are in danger of losing their lives. If one of them (probably Simon Peter) had suffered a sudden attack of smart mouth and had the advantage of the classic line from an old movie series, he might have said to Jesus what Oliver Hardy frequently said to Stan Laurel, "Well, this is another fine mess you've gotten us into!" And he would have been right. (Jesus is notorious for getting his disciples into "messes." Note these words from II Timothy 3:12: *Indeed, all who want to live a godly life in Christ Jesus will be persecuted.)*

When Steve Friedman asked his father if he had ever been scared serving as a Combat Engineer in the Italian campaign of the Second World War, Sol Friedman said, "I wasn't thinking about the bullet with my name on it. It was the one marked 'To Whom It May Concern' that worried me!"[5] Jesus didn't send his disciples into a storm on the Lake of Galilee that had their names on it; what they encountered was a "to whom it may concern" storm. Perhaps this is another implied lesson from James 4:14 (...*you do not know what tomorrow may will bring)*: You can be doing your dead-level best to live the way you sincerely believe God wants you to live and run smack dab into all kinds of "to whom it may concern" difficulties.

It would be a gross misreading of this text to draw from it the moral: stay off the lake. If you are looking for a moral from this account, it would be that when you cross the lake, be prepared for storms. Sometimes they do occur; it is the nature of the lake in this location. It is the nature of life to offer a great many "to whom it may concern" squalls that do not call for retreat, but courage. Somewhere I found the line: "Biblically, the person of faith was the person of courage who dared to venture into life." Revisiting Hebrews 11:8 provides such an illustration: *By faith, by courage, Abraham set out...."* Biblically, faith is all about setting forth, striking out, setting sail. It is never about hunkering down in a boat anchored safely on shore. (Although I understand and appreciate the metaphor, I'm not certain the disciples would have found the line from the gospel song, "I've anchored my soul in the haven of rest," an appropriate description of their lives.) I do not think it is incidental that the God who calls us to faith is the God who also issues frequent calls to courage: Deuteronomy 31:6 – *Be strong and courageous!*⁶ Courage and faith cannot be separated; it is courageous faith, rather than harbor faith, that is the real challenge. But faith is more than courage.

For so long, when I read Hebrews 12, I missed the point. I got the message that I was to be a marathon runner in the great race of a faithful life. What I misunderstood was the line *"We are surrounded by such a great cloud of witnesses."* I saw them as critical spectators. I imagined the great saints of old watching me: Abraham, Jacob, Joseph, Moses, Gideon, David, Samuel. I imagined their reminding me that I needed to be faithful and true to my calling. I already had enough people watching me and checking me out and pointing out my flaws so this just added to the number of critics already in my gallery. But this interpretation is a total misreading of the text.

These witnesses (in Hebrews 11) are witnesses to God's faithfulness. And I believe the sin *that so easily entangles us* (12:1) is our loss of confidence in the faithfulness of God. Hebrews 11 is the great roll-call of those who plead with us not to get tripped-up by that temptation. They are witnesses to God's ability to give us strength for the journey day by day. They are literally our cheering section, shouting to us each day: "Keep on going! You can make it! God was faithful to us, he will be faithful to you! Don't quit! Don't give up! Hang in there all the way to the finish line – regardless of the disappointments, failures, or setbacks!"

I found an anonymous quote I want to put in another context: "As we hang from the cliff edge waiting to fall into the arms of God, we may release nine fingers but, while one finger remains, we are still holding on." A youth group at a church where I was pastor returned from a week long summer camp and presented a video report of their experiences. One of the events of the week, that was strictly voluntary, was called "faith-fall." One person stood on a porch railing while six youth stood below with arms locked together. On signal, the person on the railing began leaning backward and fell into the human safety net below. Those who attended the camp had a visual image of the true meaning of biblical faith. Too often faith is associated with a set of beliefs, even though there is not a single passage in the New Testament in which the Greek word for faith *(pistis)* means "beliefs." John 14:1 is often translated: *Do not let your hearts be troubled. Believe in God, believe also in me.* The more accurate translation is: *Trust in God, trust also in me.* Jesus repeatedly attempts to counter the charge of the Garden of Eden tempter who maintains that God cannot be trusted. Jesus' call to a life of faith is the call to a life of trust.

Although Jesus' question to the disciples, "*Where is your faith?*" at first may seem rather foolish, it is indeed profound. When do you need more faith than when the boat is sinking? If you ever need faith, you need it then. I have always been intrigued by the confident faith demonstrated in the life of George Muller of Bristol, England. He started with two shillings in his pocket, never solicited funds, and over a period of sixty years cared for more than 10,000 orphans. One legendary episode is about the morning when Muller had no food for the large group of children gathered at the breakfast table. His words of grace were, "Father, we thank you for the food you are going to give us." Almost immediately, a baker knocked at the door with bread he had baked for the children. The second knock was from a milkman whose wagon had broken down in front of the orphanage and needed to unload cans of milk so he could take his wagon in for repairs. He asked, "Can you use the milk?" My response to those who say, "I can't believe that," is always the same: "Don't you wish you could?" The story is true and is only one of many such incredible incidents from the life of trusting George Muller. When do you need more faith than when you have absolutely nothing? When do you need faith more than when the boat is sinking?

In his version of the story, Luke omits something that Mark (an earlier version) includes. In Mark 4:40, Jesus asks his disciples, *"Why are you afraid? Have you no faith?"* Biblically, the opposite of faith is almost always posited as fear, not doubt. This sits well with the most often repeated commands in the Bible: *"Fear not! – Be not afraid!"* I have always found it interesting that there are four "fear not" messages in the stories of Advent: to Joseph (Matthew 1:20), to Zechariah (Luke 1:13), to Mary (Luke 1:30), and to the shepherds (Luke 2:10). Although I have not counted, some say there are 365 "fear nots" in the Bible, one for every day of the year.

What Jesus says to his disciples in the boat that day he says to all of his disciples at all times and under all circumstances: "You do not have to live in fear; you can live in trust and confidence in me." What I find most impressive about Jesus' admonition is that he is in the boat with his disciples when he gives it. He is not shouting encouragement from the safety of the shore.

Nevertheless, it does not escape the attention of any reader, that even though Jesus is in the boat with his disciples in the middle of the storm, he is asleep. (Sidebar: this is the only passage in the Gospels where Jesus is pictured asleep. One cannot help but be reminded of passages from the Psalms where the writer cries out to God who seems to be sleeping through their life-threatening storms.) Without, I hope, reading too much into the account, I find it most interesting that Jesus can sleep through a fierce storm but can be awakened quickly when his disciples call to him. And, sleeping or not, he was always in the boat with them. Most people find great comfort in Psalm 23 (which we will explore later) even though they seem to be unaware of its stormy aspects: *Even though I walk through the darkest valley, a valley as dark as death itself, I will fear no evil; for you are with me.* The great promise that is meant to dispel our fears is that the Lord will never forsake us, never abandon us. He will be with us on the stormy seas, in the dark valleys, in all the impossible and dangerous situations of life.

There are two questions in Luke's narrative. Jesus asks one and the disciples ask the other at the end of the story: *They said to one another, "Who is this man, that even the winds and the waves obey him?"* Well, I believe he's the one who enables you to have faith when the boat is sinking because he will never sink. He is the one who enables you to have faith when all hope is gone because he himself is our hope. He is the one who enables you to live without fear when everything is decaying and falling apart because he is the Alpha and Omega, the beginning and the end. He is the one who has pledged to journey with you all the way through life. He is the one who will be with you in that final journey over the dark and dreadful sea called death. He will take you to the other side and give you his hand as you step onto the shore of Canaan's promised-land, the land where the storms of life will be no more. And when you hear his words, "Welcome to the Father's house," you will know eternally why he really is trustworthy and why there never was any reason to be afraid – even when your boat was about to sink.

Reflections

I had several options for the title of Part I: "From Fear To Faith in An Unfinished World," "From Fear To Faith in A World Where We're Not in Charge," "From Fear to Faith in a World That Does Not Come With Operating Instructions." We live in a world as creatures; we are not the Creator. Many things are not only beyond our control but are beyond our comprehension. The confession of our common humanity is the place to begin in journeying from fear to faith.

Ann Lamott says a friend of hers begins and ends her day with the same prayers. Her morning prayer consists of "Whatever" and her prayer at the end of the day is, "Oh, well." As shocking as this first seems, these prayers are simply the expression of the realization that much of life is beyond our control and often the best we can do (and what we should do!) is cooperate with the inevitable (meaning – what comes). "Living by explanations" is not one of our options.

Job's three friends usually have a lot of company during "visitation" times at a funeral home. Overheard have been some of the most sincere and shocking pieces offered by modern "miserable comforters" (Job 16:2): "At least you have other children"; "God needed another angel"; "God never puts more on us than we can handle"; "She's so much better off now." The list is unending. My prescription for funeral home civility is a hand-clasp, a gentle hug, or, if words must be spoken, a simple, "I'm so sorry." The key is letting people be where they are in their grief and listening to what they want to say.

In the final analysis, it is our presence that is the best source of comfort. The cliché is right: showing up is 90% of everything. The powerful presence of caring people has been the source of my greatest help in times of sorrow and loss. One of the recurrent lines in an old TV series recited by the host after his advice to men segment was: "Remember, we're in this thing together." Sometimes that is all we have to offer. Perhaps, it is the best thing most of us have to offer – and to receive from others.

[1]Niles Elliot Goldstein, *God At the Edge* (New York, Bell Tower, 2000), 25.
[2]Philip Yancey, *Disappointment With God* (Grand Rapids, Zondervan Publishing House, 1998), 205.
[3]*New Living Translation* (Wheaton, Tyndale House Publishers, 1996).
[4]Kenneth S. Wuest, *The New Testament, An Expanded Translation* (Grand Rapids, William B. Eerdmans Publishing Company, 1962).
[5]Tom Brokaw, *The Greatest Generation* (New York, Random House, 1998), 383.
[6]*New International Version* (Grand Rapids, Zondervan Corporation, 1987).
[7]David Steindle-Rast, *Gratefulness, the Heart of Prayer* (New York, Paulist Press, 1984), 96.

Part I: From Fear to Faith in Our Humanity

Points to Ponder

Truth in Life 101: We can be certain of uncertainty.

The goal of the biblical story is to bring about a reversal of what happened in Eden, to bring us from fear to relational trust.

God is not in the hedge business.

The real benefit of Job's religion, the real benefit of faith, is God.

Bad things not only happen to good people, terrible things happen to wonderful people.

When you are seeking an explanation for the bad things in life, if you are not careful, you can easily make God into a devil.

Instead of attempting an explanation as to why a man is born blind, Jesus prescribes a plan of action.

Jesus didn't send his disciples into a storm on the Lake of Galilee that had their names on it; what they encountered was a "to whom it may concern" storm.

Courage and faith cannot be separated; it is courageous faith, rather than harbor faith, that is the real challenge.

"Who is this man, that even the winds and the waves obey him?"

Part II: FROM FEAR TO FAITH IN GUIDANCE

Chapter 5: The God Who Makes Promises But Doesn't Pass Out Roadmaps

MODERN OBSERVATIONS:

The Old Testament is dominated by the exodus theme – the journey out of Egypt toward the promised land, with forty years of trial and wandering....This theme of the pilgrim, the wayfarer, the traveler on a search, the knight on a quest, is a constantly recurring image of the spiritual life.[1]

Go where your best prayers take you. Unclench the fists of your spirit and take it easy. Breathe deep of the glad air and live one day at a time.[2]

When I trust deeply that today God is truly with me and holds me safe in a divine embrace, guiding every one of my steps, I can let go of my anxious need to know how tomorrow will look, or what will happen next month or next year. I can be fully where I am and pay attention to the many signs of God's love within and around me.[3]

THE BIBLICAL TEXTS: Genesis 12:1-4; Hebrews 11:8:

> Now the Lord said to Abram, "Go from your country and your kindred and your father's house to the land that I will show you. I will make of you a great nation, and I will bless you, and make your name great, so that you will be a blessing. I will bless those who bless you, and the one who curses you I will curse; and in you all the families of the earth shall be blessed." So Abram went, as the Lord had told him....By faith Abraham obeyed when

he was called to set out for a place that he was to receive as an inheritance; and he set out, not knowing where he was going.

A great many passages in Holy Scripture (like Hebrews 11:8) ought to come with a warning label: "WARNING: This text may be hazardous to spiritual tranquility. POSSIBLE SIDE-EFFECT: Increased anxiety." Far too many pronouncements about the life of faith omit what one writer calls the "thickly textured complexity" of human experience.[4] It is true that the first text (Genesis 12:1-4) speaks of a promise-making God. Note the verbs where God is the subject: *I will show, I will bless, I will make, I will curse.* This is the God who makes big promises and lays his name on the line to back them up. However, it is the companion text from Hebrews that merits the warning label; this is the God who makes promises but doesn't pass out road maps. The life of faith is far from simple; its character is also one of thickly textured complexity – even if your name is Abraham.

The immediate question from Abraham's family and friends when he announces that God has commanded him to leave town must have been, "Where are you going?" Abraham's response is, "I don't know." God has not provided Abraham with a trip-tic from the Mesopotamian Camel Club; all he does is indicate the direction in which Abraham is to travel. Many appear to have forgotten that this "not knowing" is always a part of biblical faith. (Even the Apostle Paul found intended travel plans under constant revision by the Holy Spirit and sometimes blocked by Satan, as he notes in I Thessalonians 2:18.) Abraham doesn't get much information concerning his destination; when he asks where he is going, God says, "That way." Many (most?) times in our lives as believers that is all we get

– a sense of direction. After prayer, consultation, strategic planning, and struggle, rather than handwriting on the wall or dew on the fleece (Judges 6:36-40), what we end up with is a sense of "this is what I ought to do." Rather than a fully detailed map with plainly marked hazards, possible detours, and the destination circled in red, all we often have is a gentle tug as *his Spirit bears witness with our spirit* (Romans 8:16).

Many have found comfort and encouragement from Thomas Merton's prayer:

> *My Lord God, I have no idea where I am going. I do not see the road ahead of me. I cannot know for certain where it will end. Nor do I really know myself, and the fact that I think I am following your will does not mean that I am actually doing so. But I believe that the desire to please you does in fact please you. And I hope I have that desire in all that I am doing. I hope that I will never do anything apart from that desire. And I know that if I do this, you will lead me by the right road, though I may know nothing about it. Therefore will I trust you always, though I may seem lost, and in the shadow of death. I will not fear, for you are ever with me, and you will never leave me to face my perils alone.*[5]

Psalm 109:105 is sometimes appropriated for greater assurance than it was ever meant to deliver. *Your word is a lamp to my feet and a light to my path* is encouraging reassurance that we do not have to stumble about in the darkness. Unfortunately, the kind of lamp the psalmist is talking about is not a super-powered flashlight that will dispel the darkness many yards ahead. The lamp of Psalm 119 is a simple oil lamp that will provide just enough light to enable us to take safely the next step. All too often, our problem is not that we are unaware of the next step we ought to take, but that we are concerned about something further down the road or we are worried and anxious about where we are going to wind up. (The words of Thomas Carlyle come to mind: "Our main business is not to see what lies dimly in the distance, but to do what lies clearly at hand.") Question: if you know the next step, if you know the direction in which you ought to be going, won't the final destination take care of itself? My answer is: yes, even though you may experience just what Abraham does.

Abraham does exactly what God tells him to do; he leaves his hometown with his family and starts out for what we now term "the promised-land." Just ten verses after his departure from Haran we read: *Now there was a famine in the land.* I still recall the way a seminary professor, Clyde Francisco, made this point memorable. He noted that Abraham leaves his hometown to journey to the land God has promised to give him and his descendants and when he gets there the buzzards are circling overhead. Buzzards in the promised-land! Francisco then gave us his sermon for the day: "There are always buzzards in the promised-land. That is why you have to have faith. Only faith can claim the promises of God while the buzzards are circling overhead."

While perusing the bargain section at a used bookstore, I stumbled across this arresting title: "Learning to Fall: The Blessings of an Imperfect Life." The author, Philip Simmons, at age thirty-five was diagnosed with ALS, Lou Gehrig's disease. The author gives insight into what living with this disease entails, including "laboring a quarter of an hour to spread cream cheese on a bagel." He writes:

> *The challenge is to stand at the sink with your hands in dishwater, fuming over a quarrel with your spouse, children at your back clamoring for attention, the radio blatting the bad news from Bosnia, and say, "God is here,*

now, in this room, here in this dishwater, in this dirty spoon." Don't talk to me about flowers and sunshine and waterfalls: this is the ground, here and now, in all that is ordinary and imperfect, this is the ground in which life sows the seeds of our fulfillment. The imperfect is our paradise. Let us pray, then, that we do not shun the struggle. May we attend with mindfulness, generosity, and compassion to all that is broken in our lives. May we live each flawed and too human moment and thereby gain the victory.[7]

It may seem ludicrous to talk about the blessings of an imperfect life, especially when the major imperfection is ALS. Simmons' challenge is to accept that, this side of eternity, the imperfect is our paradise, the place where struggle can lead to fulfillment and victory. When Abraham gets to the promised land it doesn't look so promising but I believe that here is where he begins to learn what real faith is all about. One of the reasons most of us want road maps for the faith-journey is so we can have some sense of certainty and control in our lives.

A reader in the Metropolitan Diary section of *The New York Times* reported an experience she had on one of her daily bus rides. She was reading an article from a magazine when she noticed, or at least suspected, that the woman seated beside her was reading along with her. As she began turning the page, her suspicion was confirmed. "Just a second," the neighbor said, "I haven't finished yet." There was a moment of silence while the magazine owner recovered her equilibrium. "I'll tell you what," she said, "I'll read at my own pace and I'll give you the magazine when I get off." There was a pause and the woman beside her said, "What if I get off first?" I dare to use this story to give some obvious McGuffey Reader morals: The travel magazine belongs to God. Don't try to get off the bus before he does, you'll get off at the wrong stop. Don't try to read over his shoulder. Don't try to take the magazine away from him; you may open it to a page that has nothing to do with his travel plans for your life.

The Garden of Eden temptation simply won't go away. Our role as dependent creatures does not sit well in an age contending that self-fulfillment, self-help, self-esteem, and an endless list of "me-isms" call for independent action. The tempter still maintains: *"If you eat of this tree of knowledge you will be like God. You will be in charge. You will be in control. You will have power. You can achieve autonomy."* When Adam and Eve make their grab for independence, they no doubt are confident they will soon be in the driver's seat of manageability. They have no idea that chaos is around the bend. Adam and Eve find what we find: life is unmanageable. We soon discover, when the ball comes right over the plate, that is the exception; when life throws us a curve it is pretty much regulation-play. In spite of our best planning, James is right; we do not know what is going to happen tomorrow. We will never be able to exercise enough control over our lives to feel secure. As you grow older, the truth that kicks in your front door is that we really can't control much of anything in our living and practically nothing in our dying. The Garden of Eden tempter is still a liar. The secret of life is not power and control; the secret of life is faith (trust) in the God who does not pass out road maps but who does indeed point in the right direction.

This necessitates reviving a major biblical metaphor for life. The story of Abraham, the story of all God's saints, reveals that life is pilgrimage, faith is pilgrimage. Life is a journey, faith is a journey - a going out. God says to Abraham, *"Go-you-forth!"* A fuller translation is: *"Get up and go!"* Literally, God's calling to Abraham in the original

Hebrew should be translated more like: *"Outgoing go out."*[8]
This underscores the often used contention that "we are
verbs, not nouns." Or, as I like to say: when you become
a noun it is all over!

A large sidebar of hope needs to be inserted for all of
us who see ourselves as far lesser persons of faith than
Abraham; next to him most of us view ourselves as spiritual
pygmies. It is helpful to contemplate that the life of faith
was no easier for Abraham than it is for us. His life was not
free from disappointments, questions, doubts, and failures.
The famine in Canaan is so severe that Abraham takes his
family down into Egypt. Evidently Sarah is still carrying
her Miss Mesopotamia Beauty Pageant crown because
Abraham fears her radiance will provoke some Egyptian to
kill him in order to get her. His remedy for such a
precarious situation is to pass off Sarah as his sister (Genesis
12:11-13). Aside from looking out for number one, putting
your wife in jeopardy, and throwing faith out the window,
it seems quite reasonable. Such flagrant trust-abuse would
no doubt have justified a negation of God's covenant
promise. But God does not cancel his contract with
Abraham even when Abraham once more misrepresents
Sarah as his sister, this time to the residents of Gerar
(Genesis 20). In the life of faith with this promise-making
God there is mercy and forgiveness and always the chance
to correct a misstep or be rescued from a foolish detour.
God's grace is just as amazing in the life of Abraham as it is
everywhere else; we depend on it just as Abraham did.
Abraham was not a perfect pilgrim but the God in whom
he trusted is the God who is perfectly trustworthy. Martin
Luther's definition of faith provides much courage and hope
for the journey: "Faith is a free surrender and a joyous
wager on the unseen, untried, and unknown goodness of
God."

The big question is always: where do you begin? Abraham begins in Haran, his hometown; that is where he was. You start where you are and however you are. How can you start from where you are not? You don't need a roadmap because God provides something better than a roadmap. The God of biblical revelation is different from any other of the gods worshiped in the ancient world. The God of the Bible is not fixated; he is not limited to location. He is the God who journeys with his people; he is the God who is on the move with his people. Some hint of just how revolutionary this idea was is revealed in Jacob's surprise when he awakes from a dreaming sleep with the cry, *"The Lord is in this place and I didn't know it!"* (Genesis 28:16).

Several years ago, I found it necessary to visit a large office building in downtown Louisville. As I got on the elevator and the door began closing, I noticed a large red button above the control panel. A sign underneath read: "In the event of an emergency push this button. Help is on the way." While I appreciated the assurance, I remembered the better message I had already received. Biblically, our sign reads: "Help is here!" God was not in the promised land waiting for Abraham to arrive. Some are shocked to discover that the term "Holy Land" is not in the Bible. According to Scripture, God is holy and the whole earth is full of his glory; the place where you are right now is holy ground. After all, the God of the Bible is not linked to places but to persons; that is why we do not speak of the God of Sinai but rather the God of Abraham, Isaac, and Jacob.

The God who points us in the right direction gives something far better than any roadmap you could ever get. It is what I call "The Great Promise" found in Matthew 28:20, the very last words in the Gospel of Matthew. Jesus says, *"Remember, I am with you always, to the end of the age."*

With this greatest promise of all, there is only one thing left for us to do: "Get going!"

Reflections

I have always used humor in my sermons. Not "jokes" or unrelated "warm-up" material. I was taught that everything in a sermon should relate to the text and no illustration should be so large or powerful that it steals the thunder from the text. The purpose of any humor is an adaptation of the Mary Poppins' song: "A little bit of laughter makes it easier to listen to the weighty texts of life." My purpose is never to offer "a spoonful of sugar" or to be perceived as giving a dose of medicine.

The Peanuts gang usually has something to offer on almost any subject. Snoopy is sitting on his doghouse thinking to himself: "Boy! When I sit up here I can see for miles....I can see the entire continent!"....With his ears up, he thinks, "I can see the whole world!"..."I can see clear over to the next yard." Our laughter enables us to admit that it is not only Snoopy who thinks he can see the whole world when in reality all he is able to do is to see into the next yard. We are not only afflicted with limited vision; we are also afflicted with distorted vision. We will deal later with Paul's confession of *seeing in a mirror dimly* (I Corinthians 13:12), but this is a succinct summary of our plight.

If we have some sense of the right direction in which to travel, that is about the best that most of us can hope for. Ever present nostalgia enables us to identify with the allegedly true story of a bishop speaking at a conference of United Methodist Ministers. At one point, he punched the air with his fist as he proclaimed, "If the 1950s ever come back again, WE'RE READY!"[9] The good news is that he was speaking facetiously; the bad news is that the statement is entirely too true for entirely too many. The journey is always forward in the faith that God is with us as he was in the past and as he will be in the future – whatever shape it may take.

[1]Francis Baur, *Life in Abundance* (New York, Paulist Press, 1983), 34.
[2]Frederick Buechner, *Telling Secrets* (New York, HarperSanFrancisco, 1992), 92.
[3]Henri J. M. Nouwen, *Here and Now* (New York, Crossroad, 1994), 33.
[4]Robert Coles, *Harvard Dairy II* (New York, Crossroad Publishing Company, 1997), 51.
[5]Thomas Merton, *No Man Is An Island* (New York, Harcourt Brace Jovanovich, 1955), 24.
[6]Philip Simmons, *Learning To Fall: The Blessings of an Imperfect Life* (New York, Bantam Books, 2002), 57.
[7]Ibid, 37.
[8]David Steindl-Rast , *Gratefulness, the Heart of Prayer*, 90.
[9]Brian McLaren and Tony Campolo, *Adventures in Missing the Point* (Grand Rapids, Zondervan, 2006), 176.

Chapter 6: God's Intention Is for Good

MODERN OBSERVATIONS:

I tend to think that any outcome of prayer that enables us to keep going is a positive answer. This view dovetails with my commitment to giving the divine mystery a blank check.[1]

...if God is love, and so we believe then love confers freedoms. While God can imagine the range of free choices we humans may make, God's love will not violate authentic freedom by programming our future. Thus, while the overall purposes of God are sure, the actual shape of a conclusion cannot be detailed with precision. God works out the divine purpose interactionally, indeed improvisationally, along with the decisions of a free-within-relationship humanity. Therefore, in our preaching, we must leave room for the improvisations of God.[2]

Romans 8:28 is surely the most astonishing verse in the Bible, for it certainly doesn't *look* as if *all* things work for good. What awful things our lives contain!...Here is the shining simplicity: *if God is total love, then everything he wills for me must come from his love and be for my good.* And if this God of sheer love is also omnipotent and can do anything he wills, then it follows that all things must work together for my ultimate good. Not necessarily for my *immediate* good, for short-range harm may be the necessary road to long-range good. And not necessarily for my *apparent* good, for appearances may be deceiving.[3]

THE BIBLICAL TEXT: Genesis 50:15-21:

> *Realizing that their father was dead, Joseph's brothers said, "What if Joseph still bears a grudge against us and pays us back in full for all the wrong that we did to him?" So they approached Joseph, saying, "Your father gave this instruction before he died, 'Say to Joseph: I beg you,*

forgive the crime of your brothers and the wrong they did in harming you.' Now therefore please forgive the crime of the servants of the God of your father." Joseph wept when they spoke to him. Then his brothers also wept, fell down before him, and said, "We are here as your slaves." But Joseph said to them, "Do not be afraid! Am I in the place of God? Even though you intended to do harm to me, God intended it for good, in order to preserve a numerous people, as he is doing today. So have no fear; I myself will provide for you and your little ones." In this way he reassured them, speaking kindly to them.

"Live and learn" doesn't appear to be the working agenda for the central family in the book of Genesis. The story of Isaac, Rebecca, Jacob, and Esau could not be titled "Father Knows Best." Even a cursive reading reveals a more appropriate caption would be "Nobody Knows Best." When Jacob becomes the head of his household it is evident that Dr. Phil has not gotten through to any of them. The continuing family story is not "Everybody Loves Joseph," but "Nobody Loves Joseph, Except Daddy." After the disastrous consequences of parental favoritism shown by Isaac to Esau and Rebecca to Jacob, you would assume that Jacob would be on the alert to make certain that same things does not occur in his family. Jacob has twelve sons and Genesis 37:3 sets the stage for family fractures: *Now (Jacob) loved Joseph more than any other of his children.*

The brothers are not required to make assumptions; Jacob does not hesitate to demonstrate Joseph's favored status. He is gifted by his father with a remarkable coat with long sleeves that has been called many things including "The Technicolor Dream Coat." Whatever its color, it was not designed for any significant hard work; it was strictly for an administrative position. Joseph parades around in his coat, flaunting his elevated status as he fulfills his role of watchdog over his brothers; he brings back regular reports to his father as to how his brothers are taking care of the family flock of sheep. Compounding his effrontery, Joseph relays to his brothers his recurring dreams in which he is promoted from watchdog to top dog and in that role they all bow down and serve him. This proves to be too much even for father Jacob (Genesis 37:10). Finally, enough is enough, and his brothers decide to kill him. Reuben's pleas prevent the murder and Judah's suggestion results in Joseph being sold as a slave to a passing caravan on its way to Egypt. The Technicolor Coat is splashed with goat's blood and presented to Jacob who, according to plan, assumes a wild animal has killed Joseph. Jacob falls into a state of permanent deep depression while Joseph falls into the role of slave in the household of Potiphar, the captain of the guard in Pharaoh's court.

I'll confess that at this point in the narrative, the cast of characters is far from exemplary. Jacob has no one but himself to blame for the hatred the brothers share for Joseph; the actions of the brothers are shocking and unforgivable; Joseph conducts himself like a spoiled brat. But when the family saga reaches its conclusion in chapter fifty, there are commendations all around, especially for Joseph who affirms: *"Even though you intended to do harm to me, God intended it for good...."* Although one can hardly imagine so much good resulting from such a dastardly deed, it is not to be imagined that the positive results issued without the cooperation of the participants. For us to realize God's intention for good in our lives, I believe it is mandatory that we use the post-pit Joseph as our mentor in his rising above anger, bitterness, and resentment.

A Texas story tells of a rancher who bought ten ranches and put them together to form one giant spread. A friend asked the name of his new mega-ranch. "It's called the Circle Q, Rambling Brook, Double Bar, Broken Circle, Crooked Creek, Golden Horseshoe, Lazy B, Bent Arrow, Sleepy T, Triple O Ranch." "Wow," exclaimed his friend, "I bet you have a lot of cattle." "Not really," lamented the rancher. "Not many survive the branding."[4] Statistics do not permit me to say "not many," but simple observation has led me to conclude that "far too many" do not survive the brandings life places on them: disappointments, setbacks, illnesses, tragedies, as well as the general unfairness and inequities that permeate all human existence. Those who don't survive such brandings don't necessarily stop breathing; they succumb to the deadly dis-eases of anger, bitterness, and resentment that quickly drain away the life qualities. When Joseph found himself a household slave down in Egypt, he could have lamented, "This is not my destiny; I'm too good for this. My dreams foreshadowed leadership, not servitude. I'll not dirty my hands on this godless Egyptian work. And just wait until I get my hands on those brothers of mine." Dale Carnegie observed, "If we rail and kick against it and grow bitter, we won't change the inevitable; but we will change ourselves. I know. I have tried it."

Cooperating with the inevitable means making the best of what cannot be changed; non-cooperation can bring a darker cast to the inevitable. Joseph doesn't rail and grow bitter. That would have been the easy way out; that would have been the tragic way out. If Joseph's days had been filled with bitterness and resentment, he would have had little energy left for productive endeavors. We only have so much energy; anger, bitterness, and resentment use up lots of it and often leave us too exhausted to invest ourselves in anything else. Genesis 39:3 tells us how Joseph uses his energy: *The Lord caused all (Joseph) did to prosper in his hands.* Joseph works. Joseph serves and so impresses his master with his efforts that he is placed in charge of the large household enterprise. Although Joseph later tells his brothers, *"Even though you intended to do harm to me, God intended it for good,"* there was one person who could have stopped the process cold – that person was Joseph. If Joseph had permitted his brothers' actions and attitudes to determine how he would act and how he would feel, the purpose and plan of God would not have been fulfilled. God's greatest gift to us, our right to choose and determine for ourselves, is also potentially our greatest source of danger. Joseph chooses not to be ruled by the things that would cause him to be less and to do less. To realize the things that God intended for good, the first thing Joseph has to do is rise above anger, bitterness, and resentment.

A part of the ability to accomplish such a difficult feat is the firm conviction that God's intention for your life is only good. The late Senator Sam Ervin often told a story that came out of the south mountain section of North Carolina. "Personal testimonies" were a part of the informal worship in many of the churches. On one occasion, Uncle Ephriam Swink, whose body was all bent and distorted with arthritis, was present for such a service. One by one the other members of the congregation stood and gave testimony to their religious experiences. Uncle Ephriam kept his seat. Finally, the pastor asked, "Uncle Ephriam, suppose you tell us what the Lord has done for you." Slowly Uncle Ephriam rose with his bent and distorted body, and said, "Brother, he has might nigh ruint me." His testimony is understandable but if anybody almost ruined Uncle Ephriam it was not God, it was Uncle Ephriam. The greatest continuing unsolved mystery is the ubiquitous evil in life. I know of no explanation for the existence of crippling arthritis but I am assured that it was not something God "sent" to Uncle Ephriam.

What Joseph tells his brothers he really believes and we ought to believe it too because it is one of the basics of biblical faith – the plan of God is for good. It is possible to translate our text: *You planned for evil, but God planned for good.* Romans 8:28 is often translated (as in the King James Version): *We know that all things work together for good.* I don't know that; often things that happen are damaging and destructive beyond repair. A better translation does not make *"all things"* the subject of the verb *works.* What I do know and believe fully is what Paul underscores in this verse with what I believe to be the correct subject of the verb *works: We know that in everything God works for good with those who love him, who are called according to his purpose.* This logically connects with Romans 8:31: *If God is for us who can be against us?* (In the Greek text there are no verbs. It makes a real impact when we read it as it is: *If God for us – who against us?*) I take the meaning of this verse to be: *Since God is for us, who can be successful against us?* God planned for good in Joseph's life and neither Joseph's brothers nor Egyptian masters could overturn God's good plan for Joseph.

This is not to say that Joseph fully understands or believes this every step of the way. As a reward for his hard work, loyalty, and integrity, Joseph finds himself imprisoned on a false charge of attempted adultery. This could hardly have seemed at the time that God was working in all things for good – but he was. Joseph must believe something because we find him such a model and efficient prisoner that he becomes overseer of the other prisoners. He may feel that his time has come when he is requested to interpret dreams for two of Pharaoh's chief officers. However, two long years pass before Joseph is remembered by the chief cupbearer. During these years Joseph works and waits and serves and grows and grows and grows. The only light during these dark prison days is recorded in Genesis 39:21: *But the Lord was with Joseph and showed him steadfast love.* Somehow (nothing is spelled out in scripture about angelic messengers or special dreams of reassurance), Joseph is aware of this; he surely reminds himself of this again and again. This must be a constant reminder for all of us. The Lord is with you...in places and situations where you cannot possibly imagine how he can intend anything good. But he does.

The Joseph we meet in the later chapters of Genesis is nothing like the tattletale, technicolor-coated brother we encountered earlier; he is now ready to solve the problem of hurt and wrong the only way it can be solved. A not-too-subtle hint of what has happened to him is revealed in the naming of his two sons (Genesis 41:51-52): *Joseph names the firstborn Manasseh, "For," he said, "God has made me forget all my hardship and all my father's house." The second he names Ephraim, "For God has made me fruitful in the land of my misfortune."*

But time has also tempered the brothers. A famine in the land of Israel finds Jacob sending his sons to buy grain in Egypt from their unrecognized brother. Puzzling maneuvers on the part of Joseph, plot twists, and a second visit to Egypt result in the dramatic episode in which Judah, who twenty-two years earlier readily agreed to sell his brother into slavery, now is prepared to remain in Egypt as a slave if Benjamin is allowed to go free. There is apparently reconciliation and reunion as Jacob and his entire family move to Egypt. But guilt has a lengthy shadow and later, when Jacob dies, the brothers fear that Joseph will take his revenge. This brings us to the scene from Genesis 50.

Everything is finally resolved the only way it can be resolved – then and now. The brothers come to Joseph and fully acknowledge what they did to him many years before was wrong; it was a crime; it was sin. They ask to be forgiven as the crying towels are passed out. These are not superficial tears but reflect the deep grief of anguish, regret, and repentance. The fractured family comes to the only possible solution for their dilemma – forgiveness. Forgiveness sets them free. Sets them free to weep and love and begin again as brothers and family.

In earlier generations, the word "revival" meant the annual church meeting of one to two weeks, usually in the summer and usually with a guest preacher. I have experienced only one real revival in my entire ministry. It occurred in a student pastorate at a rural church in northern Kentucky. It happened on the eighth day of a Sunday to Sunday revival. During the invitation hymn on that Sunday morning, a young man, Fred (not his real name) came forward and asked if he could say something to the congregation. I knew him well, so did not hesitate to honor his request. Fred faced the congregation and said, "You all know that my sister-in-law and I have not spoken for a year. I am asking for your prayers because this afternoon I want to go to her home and see if I can't make things right." The service concluded and almost everyone came by to assure this young man of their prayers. This was certainly one of the signs of real revival.

In the midst of my personal celebration, Mary, the daughter-in-law of the chair of deacons, approached me and said, "Ron, I think this is a wonderful beginning of reconciliation. I think it would also be wonderful if as Fred goes to make it right with his sister-in-law, you go to visit Sam and make it right with him." Almost everyone knew that the chair of deacons and I had some major conflicts and the relationship had been strained to say the least. My first thought to her suggestion was, "Now this is carrying revival too far!" but I said nothing and decided to talk it over at lunch.

The visiting minister was staying in the parsonage with us and during the lunch with him and my wife, Pat, I brought up the suggestion from Mary. The minister seconded the idea and said, "Pat and I will stay here and pray for you as you go to see Sam." I responded, "I have a better idea. Why don't you go and talk with Sam and Pat and I will pray for you!" They both laughed good-naturedly, but didn't take this as a viable alternative.

So, following lunch, I got in my car and drove the short distance to Sam's house. I prayed too. I prayed that he wouldn't be home! But he was. When I told him why I had come, his immediate response was, "I don't know how it happened that we got out of sorts with each other but I certainly want to do everything I can to make things right." After much talking, we agreed that during the first verse of the invitation hymn at the service that night, he would begin walking toward the front and I would begin walking toward him, we would meet and walk together to the front.

That is exactly what happened. I explained briefly to the congregation what had happened between Sam and me and that we had decided to make things right with each other. I cannot adequately describe the reaction of the congregation. They were overjoyed and the spirit in the sanctuary was not like anything I had ever experienced. But what Sam and I did was really of secondary importance. As we stood at the front and faced the congregation, seated on the second row to my right was Fred. He was seated between his brother and his sister-in-law. There wasn't a dry eye in the place and I can tell you in the words of the old gospel song, "Heaven came down and glory filled our souls." We made things right the only way you can make such things right: forgiveness of others and forgiveness of ourselves.

Elie Wiesel made a profound observation about the cast of characters in the book of Genesis: "Abraham is respected and admired, Isaac is pitied, Jacob is followed, but only Joseph is loved." As you read the story in the book of Genesis, you do conclude that Joseph comes on the scene none too soon. Things in the chosen family are really falling apart: Joseph shows up and we find forgiveness, reconciliation, grace, and love. We find the great lesson from the greatly loved Joseph. Everything that happens is certainly not good but God intends to use everything that comes our way for good. Joseph is one of the best examples I know of how to live so that we can get the good God intends for each of us.

Reflections

Believing Romans 8:28 and Genesis 50:20 is always easier in theory than in practice. Knowing they are two of the mountaintops (or bedrocks) of biblical revelation is helpful. God's will for us is good. *Every generous act of giving, with every perfect gift, is from above, coming down from the Father of lights, with whom there is no variation or shadow due to change* (James 1:17).

The corollary to this affirmation is that it therefore becomes necessary for me to master the art of letting go. Through the years I have returned again and again to the Genesis text with varying approaches and different sermon titles. Two were: "Letting Go of the Negatives of the Past In Order to Claim the Positives of the Future," and "Reframing the Past in Order to Live in the Present and Have Hope for the Future." Getting the best that God intends in the present is no easy matter.

I have struggled all my life with learning how to let

go of negative and hurtful experiences in order to move ahead. It always takes time and often helpful counsel and support. The other side to this coin is my willingness to let go of outcomes, stick to the process, and let God take care of the final results. My investment must be like that of Joseph who diligently works in spite of circumstances and the slow working out of all things for good. I am not a patient person and this has never been easy for me.

Richard Rohr writes: "All great spirituality is somehow about letting go. Trust me on this crucial point."[5] He's right. After I have done all I can do (and done it imperfectly!), what else is left except to leave things in God's hands? Nothing I can do will affect the outcome after doing all I am able to do. Why is it necessary for me to write such a statement? I need the reminder! Process is everything and that is my job. Results, outcomes, are beyond my control and are not my job. Leaving things where they belong, in the greater will and purpose of God, has got to be one of the keys for true peace.

[1]John Carmody, *How to Handle Trouble* (New York, Fawcett Columbine, 1993), 205.

[2]David Buttrick, *Preaching the New and the Now* (Louisville, Westminster John Knox Press, 1998), 123.

[3]Peter Kreef, *The God Who Loves You* (Ann Arbor, Servant Books, 1988), 8.

[4]*Homiletics*, Volume 10, Number 2, March-April, 1998, 66.

[5]Richard Rohr, *The Naked Now* (New York, Crossroad Publishing, 2001), 64.

Chapter 7: The Shepherd Who Leads in Green Pastures and Through Dark Valleys

MODERN OBSERVATIONS:

A month ago I stood in a hospital by my brother's side as the family gathered moments before he was to have a triple bypass operation to receive a new heart valve and, as things turned out, to have another valve repaired. Turning to the theologian in the family, he asked me to pray. Here was a time for me to say something profound; after all, I had studied theology most of my life. What did I say to God? Only this: "Our family has trusted you for nearly sixty years, and we are not going to stop now. Jerry's life is in your hands and in those of his surgeons. We want nothing more. Amen."[1]

However deep the pit, God's love is deeper still. Corrie ten Boom.

Never doubt in the dark what God told you in the light. Raymond Edman.

I said to the man who stood at the gate of the year: Give me a light that I may tread safely into the unknown. And he replied: Go out into the darkness, and put (your) hand into the hand of God. That shall be to (you) better than light and safer than a known way. M. Louise Haskins.

Perhaps one of the most misused and misunderstood phrases in the church today is by one of the greatest of Christian mystics, St. John of the Cross – "dark night of the soul." Pastors use it in their teaching to describe a phase of the soul that is the equivalent of "walking through the valley of the shadow of death," but St. John's "dark night" is neither a psychological nor pathological phase of the Christian life. It is his symbol for the entire journey of faith. "Those who enter the night never leave it, though the night changes."[2]

THE BIBLICAL TEXT: Psalm 23:1-2, 4a:

> *The Lord is my shepherd, I shall not want. He makes me lie down in green pastures; he leads me beside still waters....Even though I walk through the darkest valley, I fear no evil; for you are with me.*

It is known as the world's favorite psalm. Why shouldn't it be? Just hearing the words *The Lord is my shepherd* is like a dose of tranquility. What better way could there be to begin the day with calm reassurance than to read various translations of this never out of date metaphor: *The Eternal shepherds me, I lack for nothing.*[3] *In grassy meadows he lets me lie. By tranquil streams he leads me.*[4]

If you want to retain a peaceful spirit it is best to stop reading after the second sentence of Psalm 23. Verse three states that a major part of God's agenda as shepherd is leading in paths of righteousness or justice; this involves the flock's participation in making certain that the Divine will is done on earth as it is in heaven. (Just as Jesus taught his disciples to pray). No passive tranquility here and certainly a journey into high risk territory for the sheep. Alarm bells continue to ring when the psalmist declares that this great shepherd who blesses his sheep with green pastures and still waters may a short time later be found leading them through the darkest valley. The shepherd may be jeopardizing his leadership role; when his contract comes up for renewal, the sheep may vote for somebody who has better grazing arrangements. What kind of a shepherd is this anyway? What kind of strategy does he have in mind for his flock? The King James translation of this valley is *the valley of the shadow of death.* Other possible translations include: *a glen of gloom; a ravine as dark as death; a valley of darkness; a valley of shadows; the darkest valley.* All of these designate a place you don't want to be. In the context of the psalm, it would be the place where robbers and wild animals are waiting to pounce on helpless, defenseless sheep.

"*What's Up Doc?*" is one of my four-star favorite movies. In a courtroom scene, the judge is hearing testimony from various individuals about a confusing and chaotic episode. After one person feebly attempts to describe the events, the judge continues to look puzzled and finally says, "Let's skip over that part." The enigmatic part that is skipped over turns out to be the key to everything that happened. Too many want to skip over the dark valley portion of Psalm 23; I believe the key to the psalm is found in this dark valley, and, in reality, the attempt to bypass it is impossible.

William Blake's words may seem archaic but the concept is not:

> *Joy and woe are woven fine,*
> *A clothing for the soul devine.*
> *Under every grief and pine*
> *Runs a joy with silken twine.*
> *It is right it should be so;*
> *We were made for joy and woe;*
> *And when this we rightly know,*
> *Through the world we safely go.*

Joy and grief are a part of every life just as grassy meadows, quiet waters, and dark valleys are a part of the life of sheep, even sheep who have the Lord as their shepherd. Too much modern self-fulfillment, positive-thinking faith makes far too small a place for darkness, difficulty, and suffering. Some skip over it all together. However meritorious, I don't believe the only kind of worship I could experience is "praise worship." Sometimes life hits you and those you love (and the world) with such a vengeance that praise is the last thing you are able to do. The psalmist knows what every person who lives with operating reality checks knows: divine leadership in the life of faith includes sometimes finding one's self in the darkest valley imaginable. The reason the psalmist contends he is unafraid is not because God turns on all the lights.

Even though I walk through the darkest valley, I will fear no evil; for you are with me. This is the central affirmation of the psalmist; the writer underscores the fact by the change in pronouns: *He makes me lie down in green pastures; He leads me beside the still waters; He restores my soul; He leads me in the right paths; I fear no evil for YOU are with me.* This is the focus of the psalm. The opening verse has an implied declaration: *The Lord is my shepherd, therefore I lack nothing because He is the one real necessity of life!* What are sheep without a shepherd? Everything else is secondary to this essential priority; everything else comes because the sheep have a shepherd.

There are many reasons for the success of the 1997 *Titanic* movie. The story, of course, is unforgettable; it is supposedly one of the three most written about subjects (the other two: Jesus and the Civil War). The incredible special effects in *Titanic* cannot account for the explosive box-office receipts. The fictional love story contained that element everyone is looking for: in the midst of danger and uncertainty we hear the words, "Take my hand; I won't let you go." In the darkest valley, on the S. S. Titanic, or wherever, we do not have to be afraid because the Lord is with us in the way that Jesus reminds us in John 10:27-29:

> *My sheep hear my voice. I know them, and they follow*
> *me. I give them eternal life, and they will never perish.*
> *No one will snatch them out of my hand. What my*
> *Father has given me is greater than all else, and no one*

can snatch it out of the Father's hand.

We need constant reminders that the perfection offering such security belongs to the shepherd, not to the sheep. Phyllis McGinley opines: "The wonderful thing about saints is that they are human. They lost their tempers, they scolded God, were egotistical or testy or impatient in their turns, made mistakes and regretted them. Still they went on doggedly blundering toward heaven."[6] "Doggedly blundering toward heaven" is a classic way to describe most of us (including the best of us) making the journey as a part of God's flock. In *The Cloister Walk*, Kathleen Norris describes life in a Benedictine monastery. She tells of two eighty-year-old monks who told her about legendary falls sustained by monks of the community:

> *It was an impressive collection: falls off roofs and falls from trees, falls over tree roots in the woods, falls into quicksand. The two (eighty-year-olds) were wily, cagey, telling stories about each other that had obviously been well-polished over the years. "He fell down on the ice," one said, pointing to the other, "and he lay on the frozen lake for over an hour before anyone found him, and in all that time he never had one pious thought."*[7]

Of course not! Who could possibly think pious thoughts while shivering on a sheet of ice? But he was still doggedly blundering toward heaven! Who can continually think pious thoughts while in a deep, dark valley? Job didn't. Moses didn't. Too many of God's best saints unmercifully chastise themselves for wondering and questioning and complaining and fussing. (The writers of the psalms harbor no such reservations.) Even during times free from pious thoughts you can continue blundering in the right direction.

After all, the major point of the entire psalm is: *He leads me.* The verb translated *leads* is a powerful word. The two Hebrew words translated *leads* in verses two and three occur together in Exodus 15:13 in a song celebrating the exodus. The *"He"* who leads is no less than the God of the exodus who led his people out of bondage into "a land flowing with milk and honey." This shepherd of ours is no Johnny-come-lately; this is the Shepherd God of rescue and deliverance. This is the God who can make a way through the sea, bring water from a rock in the wilderness, and abundantly supply daily manna. The real issue raised in this psalm is the pervasive issue throughout scripture: will you trust the God who shepherds you to grassy meadows, quiet streams, and through dark valleys? The trust motif is everywhere in the psalms. Here are a few examples:

> 25:2: *O my God, in you I trust.*
> 28:7: *The Lord is my strength and my shield; in him my heart trusts.*
> 32:10: *Many are the torments of the wicked, but steadfast love surrounds those who trust in the Lord.*
> 56:11: *In God I trust; I am not afraid. What can a mere mortal do to me.*
> 31:14-15: *...I trust in you, O Lord; I say, You are my God." My times are in your hand....*

Our trust is in one whose leadership is corrective, redemptive, and restorative: *...he leads me beside still waters; he restores my soul.* Other possible translations are: *By tranquil streams he leads me to restore my spirit.*[8] *He leads me to refreshing streams, he revives life in me.*[9] Some commentators insist that the purpose of this psalm is not to communicate a sense of peace and tranquility but to emphasize that God keeps the psalmist alive,[10] keeps him alive even in the darkest valleys.

The next time you read Psalm 23, instead of reading *The Lord is my shepherd*, put your name in place of the pronoun. Find yourself in Psalm 23; especially in the last verse: *Surely goodness and mercy (or love) will follow me all the days of my life, and I will dwell in the house of the Lord forever.* The true meaning of the Hebrew verb is not reflected in the English translation *will follow me;* it is better (and more accurately) translated *pursue: Surely goodness and mercy will pursue me all the days of my life.* An unknown Scottish preacher reflected on this psalm: "The Lord is my shepherd, aye, and he has two fine Collie dogs, goodness and mercy. They will see us safely home."[11]

Reflections

I wish I knew the source of this anonymous quote: "Adversity introduces us to ourselves." I also wish that it weren't true. If all of my life had been lived in green pastures beside still waters I would know far less about myself than I do now – which is still not nearly enough! I needed those dark valleys. They provided me with the best times for reflection I have ever known.

It never really happened, but I will sometimes confess in a sermon on spiritual growth that my prayer at the beginning of my journey was: "Lord, put me in a comfortable hammock somewhere on a beautiful beach, with warm breezes blowing over me, a cold glass of lemonade in my hand, and make me into a saint!" It always gets a smile from people who know a truth difficult to take any other way. The road to maturity is the road of great difficulty.

Pilgrim's Progress is probably not widely read these days (and may not even be widely known). Philip Yancey makes this observation:

> *John Bunyan's version of the Christian life differs from what I read in most Christian books today. Every few pages the pilgrim makes some stupid mistake and nearly loses his life. He takes wrong turns and detours. His only companion sinks in the Slough of Despond. The pilgrim yields to worldly temptations. He flirts with suicide and decides again and again to abandon the quest. At one such moment, Mr. Hopeful assures him, "Be of good cheer, my brother, for I feel the bottom, and it is sound." Acting in courageous faith, the pilgrim continues his journey and in the end arrives at his destination, the Celestial City.*[12]

At one time *Pilgrim's Progress* sold more copies than any other book except for the Bible. Wonder why that isn't true today?

[1]James L. Crenshaw, *Trembling at the Threshold of a Biblical Text* (Grand Rapids, William B. Eerdmans Publishing Company, 1994), 22.
[2]Leonard Sweet, *A Cup of Coffee at the Soul Café* (Nashville, Broadman & Holman Publishers, 1998), 55.
[3]James Moffat, *A New Translation of the Bible* (New York, Harper & Row, 1954).
[4]*The New Jerusalem Bible* (New York, Doubleday, 1985).
[5]Adapted from *The Interpreter's Bible*, Volume IV (Nashville, Abingdon Press, 1996), 66.
[6]James Cox, ed., *Best Sermons 4* (New York, HarperSanFrancisco, 1991), 119.
[7]Kathleen Norris, *The Cloister Walk* (New York, Riverhead Books, 1996), 339.
[8]*The New Jerusalem Bible* (New York, Doubleday, 1985).
[9]James Moffat, *A New Translation of the Bible* (New York, Harper & Row, 1954).
[10]*The New Interpreter's Bible, Volume IV,* (Nashville, Abingdon Press, 1996), 767.
[11]Thomas David Austin, *Faith Journey of a Pilgrim* (Macon, Smyth & Helwys, 2000), p. 131.
[12]Philip Yancey, *Reaching for the Invisible God* (Grand Rapids,

Zondervan Publishing House, 2000), 93.

Chapter 8: The Future: Closed or Open?

MODERN OBSERVATIONS:

Practically, a God of eternally static certainties is incapable of interacting with humans in a relevant way. The God of the possible, by contrast, is a God who can work with us to truly change what *might* have been into what *should* be.[1]

He says here (Jeremiah 18:7-10), "*I change my mind.*" How could he say it any clearer? If this passage doesn't teach us that God can truly change his intentions, what would a passage that *did* teach this look like?[2]

...chaos theory, combined with quantum theory gives a one-two punch to the old deterministic model of a closed universe....The laws of physics still work, but in the context of a wide-open system that has been dubbed "chaotic." One need no longer do logical gymnastics to make a case for the intervention of God into the old closed universe of Newton. Instead, chaos theory suggests that the universe is not closed at all, but wide open for God to interact with creation from the subatomic to the cosmic levels. Rather than thinking of the intervention of God and the suspension of the laws of nature, chaos theory suggests an open universe in which God has freedom of expression.[3]

THE BIBLICAL TEXT: II Kings 20:1-6:

> *In those days Hezekiah became sick and was at the point of death. The prophet Isaiah son of Amoz came to him, and said to him, "Thus says the Lord: Set your house in order, for you shall die; you shall not recover." Then Hezekiah turned his face to the wall and prayed to the Lord: "Remember now, O Lord, I implore you, how I*

have walked before you in faithfulness with a whole heart, and have done what is good in your sight." Hezekiah wept bitterly. Before Isaiah had gone out of the middle court, the word of the Lord came to him: "Turn back, and say to Hezekiah prince of my people, Thus says the Lord, the God of your ancestor David: I have heard your prayer, I have seen your tears; indeed, I will heal you; on the third day you shall go up to the house of the Lord. I will add fifteen years to your life. I will deliver you and this city out of the hand of the king of Assyria; I will defend this city for my own sake and for my servant David's sake."

If you take this text at face value, it threatens to undermine some widely accepted assumptions about life. Like the one I've heard all my life: "You won't go 'till your number comes up." Well, here is a story about a man whose number comes up, he prays, and God gives him another number. For those who maintain another interpretation explains what this story "really means," my challenge is: not if you believe the truth of the account. Not if you believe that truth is often underscored in scripture by repetition. In case you overlook the account in II Kings 20, it is repeated in Isaiah 38. It is almost as though the Bible is shouting, "Now hear this!"

It is not something easily heard because we have heard other things that color our thinking about this issue. The first rule in sermon preparation (and biblical study) is: listen to the text. Don't attempt to impose something on the text that isn't there. Let the text speak for itself regardless of how strange it sounds. Martin Luther maintained that "the Bible is the voice of revelation not to be confused with, encumbered by, or contained in any human categories of interpretation that make the voice more coherent, domesticated, or palatable." A noted scholar cites this quotation and comments: "Luther's primary passion (was) that Scripture have its own voice, to be heard in its own liberated radicality."[4] Even though it does not address the many ramifications of a doctrine of predestination, if we listen to this text in its undomesticated and radical rawness, we are led to some definite deductions.

My immediate reaction to the story in II Kings 20 is that it certainly doesn't sound like *"Que Sera Sera"* to me. The line from the old song runs: "Que sera sera, whatever will be, will be; the future's not ours to see, que sera sera." This philosophy is a form of fatalism. It is the idea that your life is like a TV show (for some of us it might be compared to a sitcom!) that has already been filmed and is simply being played out. I maintain that this is an unbiblical idea and often results in all sorts of life-twisting maneuvers, as illustrated in this anecdote: A young lad burst into his mother's drawing room, crying, "Ma, I caught a toad, and I bashed him and jumped on him and ran over him with the lawnmower 'till...." Suddenly he looked around and saw that the minister was visiting in the home. He quickly added, "...'till God called him home."[5] In this piece of humorous fiction, the obvious punch line is that the fate of the toad had more to do with a boy and a lawnmower that it did with the call of God.

This is not to say there is nothing about God's plans and purposes in scripture. In the Old Testament, the Hebrew word *hsb* can be rendered "plan." This was cited in Genesis 50:20: *Even though you planned (hsb) to do harm to me, God planned (hsb) it for good....* " I agree with the writer who sees this as an "enduring intentionality" and not a predetermined and foreordained set of specific occurrences.[6]

I understand this to mean that God's ultimate purposes of redemption will not be thwarted. The book of Revelation assures us that God's powerful intentionality will result in a new heaven and a new earth. Evil will not ultimately win out over good. Hate will not triumph over love. Falsehood will not ultimately destroy the truth. Death will not ultimately have the last word; God will have the last word and his last word is life.

In spite of other interpretations, I suggest that when the word *predestined* is used in scripture, it can almost always be read as having to do with God's enduring intentionality. Ephesians 1:5: *He predestined us for adoption as his children through Jesus Christ.* What was predestined was the method, the way, through which God would bring his erring creation back to himself. Romans 8:29: *For those whom he foreknew he also predestined to be conformed to the image of his Son, in order that he might be the firstborn with a large family.* What was predestined is what God's children are to look like; they are to look like Jesus! (I confess that it would take another book to deal adequately with this verse.)

This predestination is not a *que sera sera* fixed future event such as reported in a *New York Times* Metropolitan Diary story. A mother and her four-year-old son were on a plane awaiting takeoff for a long anticipated trip to Disney World. The child had expressed his fear of flying but at the moment was chattering excitedly about his soon-to-be-realized adventure. He suddenly fell silent. His mother noticed he had clenched his fists and squeezed his eyes shut. "What are you doing?" she asked. "I'm praying," he said. When she inquired, "About what?" he replied, "that if the plane has to crash, it be on the way home." Of course, there is no inevitable crash prerecorded in a *que sera sera* future. Our text reveals that the future has a surprising aspect of openness.

God sends the prophet Isaiah to tell King Hezekiah to set his affairs in order; his present illness will prove fatal. Isaiah delivers the message and Hezekiah prays. Before Isaiah gets out of the palace, God's word comes to him, "Go back and tell Hezekiah that things have changed. I am adding another fifteen years to his life." A prophet carries a direct word from the Lord about a certain future event. Hezekiah prays and the future is changed. One commentary heads this section: "The Power of Prayer."[7] God instructs Isaiah to tell Hezekiah: *"I have HEARD your prayer, I have SEEN your tears; indeed, I will HEAL YOU.....I will ADD fifteen years to your life. I will DELIVER you and this city out of the hand of the king of Assyria; I will DEFEND this city for my own sake and for my servant David's sake* (emphasis mine). I don't pretend to begin to understand all that is going on here. What I do know is that when Hezekiah prays, God hears, sees, and pledges to add to his life and deliver the city. Big question: would this have happened if Hezekiah had not prayed? According to the account, Hezekiah does pray and things change. (I am well aware of the many righteous persons whose earnest and tearful prayers have not resulted in situational change. Philip Yancey deals with issues like this in his excellent book *Where Is God When It Hurts?*)

If the future is fixed, determined, and closed, what do you do with James 5:14-16?:

> *Are any among you sick? They should call for the elders of the church and have them pray over them, anointing*

*them with oil in the name of the Lord. The prayer of
faith will save the sick, and the Lord will raise them up;
and anyone who has committed sins will be forgiven.
Therefore confess your sins to one another, and pray for
one another, so that you may be healed. The prayer of the
righteous is powerful and effective.*

According to this passage, the future is far more
open than many of us would like to admit. If the future is
as open as the Bible indicates, we are not victims. We have
much to do with what the future holds for us as
Shakespeare's Cassius reminds us: "The fault, dear Brutus,
is not in our stars, But in ourselves, that we are underlings."[8]
Our fate is not fixed in some distant constellation. We
don't discover which way the daily cookie is going to
crumble by referencing a newspaper horoscope. Those
great and awesome words relating to God's creating human
beings in his own image come to mind: free will, choice,
discretion, option, initiative, responsibility. Even taking
into account the givens of time, circumstances, genes, etc.,
there remains a world of possibilities. This insightful
observation comes from *Ten Thoughts to Take Into Eternity:*

> *When, during a dicey period in my life, I entered group
> therapy, I was struck by the scant perspective that people
> (including me) have on their troubles. Most unhappy
> people feel trapped for one reason alone: they are
> unaware of the options that might liberate them. They
> are their own jailers, pacing the prison cells of their lives,
> stewing in their own juices, cautiously hewing to the
> cowardly dictum "Better the devil you know...." Instead
> of exercising their constitutional right to pursue
> happiness, they rest on a treadmill that has stalled.[9]*

I want to set another quote from *Recapture Your*

Dreams next to that one and then cite a biblical example:

> *Most of the time we are not allowed to choose whether or not we will be dealt severe blows in life. What we can choose is whether we will stay down for the count or get up – and keep getting up – again and again. You can dream again. There is a future for you.*[10]

In Chapter 6, we touched on Joseph's story, his being thrown into a cistern, sold into slavery, spending years in prison. Clyde Francisco had a favorite line he used about Joseph's response to all that happened to him: "Joseph was just like cream; he always rose to the top." That was because he didn't stay down for the count; he did not stew in his own juice; he did not rest on a treadmill that had stalled; he didn't feel trapped because he felt he had no options. He remembered his dreams and he continued to dream. All of this was a part of Joseph's faith-stance.

The hot-debates and prolific publications notwithstanding, II Kings 20:1-6 has two specific text-truths: Hezekiah's future was different because he prayed; the future God was working with was different because he responded to Hezekiah's prayer. Romans 8:28 immediately comes to mind: *And we know that in everything God cooperates for good with those who love him and who are called according to his purpose.* I view this as an open invitation from God who says to each of us: "Let's see what you and I can make of the future. After all, we're in this thing together." For me, this means a future open to all kinds of wonderful possibilities...both now...and eternally.

Reflections

The subject of Chapter 8 is one of the hottest subjects under discussion today and many people have gotten burned in the process of offering their convictions. It needs to be stated again that sincere and devout persons who earnestly, thoughtfully, prayerfully, and studiously pore over the scriptures under what they truly believe to be the guidance of the Spirit, come to honest differences of opinion as to the meaning of various texts. It is not a matter of those who believe the Bible and those who don't. Often in Bible studies, I will say, "This text as I understand (interpret) it, teaches us...." I don't expect everyone to come out where I do but I do not grant anyone the right to say that because I differ from them that I don't really believe the Bible.

Whether you label it "Calvinism" or "predestination" or "Open Theism," you've got a hot potato in your hands. I have no method or plan or intention for resolving the complex issue of holding together the sovereignty of God and our free will (ability to choose). Even the Reformers walked the tightrope of proclaiming God's sovereignty (loudly and strongly) without falling into fatalism. The bottom line: if it's already decided, what can I do about it? If it's all predetermined, I'm just a victim.

All I know is that there are enough indications in scripture to convince me that things are not nearly as "fixed" as some would have us believe. Although the passages can be translated in various ways, all the meanings convey the same message. After the golden calf episode in Exodus 32, God tells Moses: *I have seen this people, how still-necked they are. Now let me alone, so that my wrath may burn hot against them and I may consume them; and of you I will make a great nation.*" But Moses does not let God alone. He makes his case (a very strong one) for God's not destroying his people. Moses asks God to *change his mind* (32:12). Exodus 32:14 reads: *And the Lord changed his mind about the disaster that he planned to bring on his people.* The NIV translates: *Then the Lord relented and did not bring on his people the disaster he had threatened.*

The plain meaning of the text is that the prayer of Moses brought about a change in what God was going to do; the future was different from what it might have been. As God gives Jeremiah his call to preach to the people, he says (Jeremiah 26:2b-3):...*speak to them all the words that I command you; do not hold back a word. It may be that they will listen, all of them, and will turn from their evil way, that I may change my mind about the disaster that I intend to bring on them because of their evil doings.* After Jonah preaches to the people in Nineveh and gives them God's forty-day warning, the king issues a decree that concludes with: *Who knows? God may relent and change his mind; he may turn from his fierce anger, so that we do not perish* (3:9). The next verse reads: *When God saw what they did, how they turned from their evil ways, God changed his mind about the calamity that he had said he would bring upon them; and he did not do it* (3:10).

These passages indicate that God responds to prayers (and changed behavior) and makes a new future. In the Old Testament, there are more passages than I can count that contain the important word "if." That "if" tells me that the ultimate purpose of God for the triumph of his Kingdom in all its fullness, does not mean that we live in a world where *everything* is predetermined. We still have a whole lot to do with the kind of future that unfolds in our lives.

[1]Gregory A. Boyd, *God of the Possible* (Grand Rapids, Baker Books, 2000), 18.

[2]Ibid. 78.

[3]Harry Lee Poe, *Christian Witness in a Postmodern World* (Nashville, Abingdon, 2000), 122.

[4]Walter Brueggemann, *Theology of the Old Testament* (Minneapolis, Fortress Press, 1997), 3.

[5]Robertson Davies, *The Merry Heart* (New York, Viking, 1996), 202.

[6]Walter Brueggemann, *Theology of the Old Testament,* 355.

[7]Christopher R. Seitz, *Isaiah 1-39, Interpretation* (Louisville, John Knox Press, 1993), 254.

[8]*Julius Caesar,* Act I, Scene I, Line 40.

[9]David Yount, *Ten Thoughts To Take Into Eternity* (New York, Simon & Schuster, 1999), 74.

[10]David Shibley, *Recapturing Your Dreams* (Green Forest, AR, New Leaf Press, 1988), 18.

Part II: From Fear to Faith in Guidance

Points to Ponder

God does not provide Abraham with a trip-tic from the Mesopotamian Camel Club; all he does is indicate the direction in which Abraham is to travel.

If you know the next step, if you know the direction in which you ought to be going, won't the final destination take care of itself?

We are verbs, not nouns. When you become a noun it is all over.

Cooperating with the inevitable means making the best of what cannot be changed.

The subject of the verb *works* in Romans 8:28 is *God*, not *everything. We know that in everything God works for the good with those who love him, who are called according to his purpose.*

Joseph is one of the best examples of how to live so that we can get the good that God intends for our lives.

If the Lord is your shepherd, why would he ever lead you through the darkest valley?

The reason the psalmist (in Psalm 23) contends he is unafraid in the dark valley is not because God turns on all the lights.

Our trust is in One whose leadership is corrective, redemptive, and restorative.

II Kings 20 contains the story about a man whose number comes up, he prays, and God gives him another number.

What is predestined is what God's children are to look like; they are to look like Jesus.

If the future is as open as the Bible seems to indicate, we are not victims.

Part III: From Fear to Faith in God's Ways

Chapter 9: Why Would Anyone Ask Jesus To Get Out of Town?

MODERN OBSERVATIONS:

Jesus' approach to "unclean" people dismayed his countrymen and, in the end, helped to get him crucified. In essence, Jesus canceled the cherished principle of the Old Testament, No Oddballs Allowed, replacing it with a new rule of grace: "We're all oddballs, but God loves us anyhow."[1]

Reflect upon the times when Christ himself stated priorities....Of the man on his way to church with hatred in his heart for someone: "*First* be reconciled to your brother, and only then come and offer your gift at the altar." To those whose delight it was to see faults and sins in others: "*First* take the plank out of your own eye and then you will see clearly to take the speck out of your brother's eye." To the rich young man who wanted to be with him: "*First* sell what you have, and give to the poor." To those who found the woman in the act of adultery: "Let him who is without sin cast the *first* stone." To self-righteous Pharisees: "*First* clean the inside of the cup, then the outside will be clean also."[2]

The divine is present in the world in complex ways. The notion that you're going to have an ordered and orderly life as a disciple of Jesus Christ is bunk. You want a conventional, convenient, consistent, predictable life? Then don't follow Jesus. There is a complexity of referents if you're a Christian. For the disciple of Jesus, God can be present in tragedies, defeats, conflicts, and crucifixions as in victories, successes, and resurrections....You follow Jesus, and you *will* be tried, and you *will* be tested.[3]

THE BIBLICAL TEXT: Mark 5:14-17 (NIV):

> *Those tending the pigs ran off and reported this in the town and countryside, and the people went out to see what had happened. When they came to Jesus, they saw the man who had been possessed by the legion of demons, sitting there, dressed and in his right mind; and they were afraid. Those who had seen it told the people what had happened to the demon possessed man – and told about the pigs as well. Then the people began to plead with Jesus to leave their region.*[4]

The day begins like a Norman Rockwell painting: Jesus is at the lakeside where a crowd has gathered around him. The day ends like an Alfred Hitchcock movie: Jesus and his disciples encounter a shrieking maniac in a cemetery. The day begins with Jesus telling stories; when the day is over the disciples have quite a story to tell, although in Mark's lengthy narrative there is not a single word from them. Even Peter seems to have nothing to say. For the disciple who usually has a comment on everything, he seems to join the others in open-mouthed stupefaction.

Let me briefly set the stage for our text. Toward evening, after a day of parabolic teaching, both publicly to a sizeable crowd and privately to his disciples, Jesus requests that they go across the lake (Galilee). At some point during the two-hour trip, a violent storm erupts and even experienced fishermen fear for their lives. An exhausted, sleeping Jesus is awakened; he rebukes the storm and the wind ceases; he rebukes his disciples for being possessed with fear instead of faith and they are thunderstruck with astonishment. Those of us familiar with the gospel narrative can echo the old show business cliché: "They ain't seen nothin' yet!"

As Jesus steps out of the boat on the other side of the lake, a shrieking, naked man emerges from the shadowy twilight of a graveyard. He races to Jesus and throws himself at his feet. The encounter concludes with a large crowd emerging from the city to find the man sitting beside Jesus, clothed and in his right mind. "You would think they would have given him the key to the city. Instead they suggest a bus ticket out of town....But why?"[5] My question exactly. Why would anyone, much less an entire populace, ask Jesus to get out of town? If we quickly leap to harsh judgment toward these anonymous townsfolk, we can easily miss spotting ourselves among their number. (Is not one major tenant of productive Bible study to find ourselves in the narratives? And identifying not just with the "good" folks?) In a careful reading of Mark's gospel, we may discover that we are just as disturbed by what Jesus does as they are. We may also discover that a careful reading of scripture is far from easy.

Miriam "Ma" Ferguson was elected governor of Texas in 1924. There was an intense debate about whether Spanish should be used in the public schools by children who had recently moved from Mexico. Governor Ferguson opposed the use of Spanish; she concluded her argument by holding up a Bible and saying, "If English was good enough for Jesus Christ, it's good enough for Texans!"[6]   Contrary to popular opinion, the Bible in the hands of many is a lethal weapon, lethal to common sense, civility, and theological truth. (Reminder: the Bible was not written in English and published by Harper and Row. The faithful in Jesus' day read from Hebrew scripture texts; Jesus spoke Aramaic; the Gospel of Mark was written in Greek; we are reading it in an English translation.) Needless to say, I think we can come to greater truth than Governor Ferguson did. The specifics of the narrative and some knowledge of the cultural and social context are essential ingredients in a careful reading.

The howling lunatic who meets Jesus is wearing only pieces of chain, evidence that attempts to subdue him have all met with failure. Even Jesus' first attempt at healing does not succeed; he commands the unclean spirit to come out of the man and nothing happens (5:7-8). Jesus asks for a name and the reply is, "Legion." A Roman legion was a regiment of 6,000 troops; Jesus asks the man his name and he gives a number, making "The Three Faces of Eve" pale to insignificance. The immediate request of the demons is for permission to enter a large herd of pigs on the nearby hillside. (This is Gentile territory; the presence of pigs is not unusual.) Jesus grants the request, the demons enter the pigs, and the herd of about 2,000 rushes down the steep bank and is drowned in the lake. This is the only incident in any of the gospels where Jesus is involved in the destruction of property.   Many commentators are convinced a part of the possessed man's cure was this demonstration that the demons had gone out of him. This water destruction brings to mind the scene from *The Wizard of Oz* when Dorothy accidentally throws water on the wicked witch and she melts away. In Jesus' day it was a common belief that demons were dry-land creatures who didn't go near water; most held that deep water was the only way to get rid of demons. In more recent times, a sailor working on a ship at the waterline was said to be "between the devil and the deep blue sea."[7] What is significant is that the man is healed; in the process of healing Jesus upsets the neighborhood.

The chagrin is understandable. There were probably multiple owners of the herd of pigs feeding on the hillside; the owners hired men to care for the animals and keep them out of the city. It was a profitable arrangement that worked well until Jesus showed up. When the pig keepers fled back into town, in a modern context, they might have reported, "You'll never guess what happened! Your IRAs just ran over the cliff!" I find no readily acceptable explanation for all that country ham dashing to a watery ruin. The real value in this story is not in finding answers but in searching for relevant questions. Questions like: Why weren't the people rejoicing that a mentally deranged man has been healed, regardless of how it happened? If the issue on the ballot that day had been "Pigs or People?" how would they (we) have voted? Regrettably, an appropriate motel door sign, "Do Not Disturb," all too frequently appears in the life of faith. *"Comfort, O comfort my people,"* says your God (Isaiah 40:1) is usually not the first (and certainly not the only) word from the Lord. The comfort most frequently comes to those on the other side of extreme difficulties or outright tragedy. The initial words to Jesus from the Gerasene Demoniac, shouted at the top of his voice, are: *"What do you have to do with me, Jesus, Son of the*

Most High God? I adjure you by God, do not torment me"
(5:7).

We know that Jesus' purpose is not further agony;
you really stop to wonder how the demoniac's situation
could be any worse. Jesus wants to heal him, to release him,
to restore him, even if that means initial additional anxiety.
Disturbing issues that must be faced and discomforting
changes that must be made are most often the prerequisites
to the comfort we seek. *"Peace! Be still!"* (Mark 4:39) is
most often heard only after we have been battered by a
terrible storm of hurricane proportions. The call for
comfort, a challenge-free faith, and simplicity in everything
is a call to which the church must not respond. Dallas
Willard makes this observation:

> *In...our longing for goodness and rightness and
> acceptance and orientation (we) cling to bumper
> slogans...that make no sense. "Stand up for your rights"
> sounds so good. How about: "All I ever needed to know
> I learned in kindergarten?" And "Practice random
> kindnesses and senseless acts of beauty"? And so forth.*

> *Such sayings contain a tiny element of truth. But if you
> try to actually plan your life using them you are
> immediately in deep, deep trouble. They will lead you
> 180 degrees in the wrong direction....But try instead:
> "Stand up for your responsibilities" or "I don't know
> what I need to know and must now devote my full
> attention and strength to finding out" (consider Proverbs
> 3:7 or 4:7) or "Practice routinely purposeful kindnesses
> and intelligent acts of beauty."*

> *Putting these into practice immediately begins to bring
> truth, goodness, strength, and beauty into our lives.*[7]

But we'll never achieve any of these things if we have

a "Do Not Disturb" sign hanging on our lives.

From an anonymous source file comes the (admittedly outrageous) story of the man, obviously intoxicated, making his uncertain way down the street, when he is spotted by a friend who approaches him and immediately notices large blisters on both of his ears. "What happened to you?" he asks. "Oh," the man replies, "my wife left her iron on and when the phone rang I picked up the iron by mistake." "Yes, but what about the other ear?" With obvious anger the man returned, "The stupid fool called back!" Was the problem that the iron should have carried a tag, "Warning: this iron does not ring?"

Most observers wouldn't need more than two seconds to conclude that the man's problem was not with the person who called or the iron, or the telephone. He needed to think about his problem in a new way; he needed to repent. Repentance is a central idea in the gospels; it is the initial message of both John the Baptist and Jesus. It is not so much sorrow for past actions and attitudes as it is the decision for a change of direction and a change of mind. It involves going a new way AND thinking a new way. "Indeed, the call of Jesus "to repent" is nothing but a call to think about how we have been thinking."[8] Two of Jesus' methods to get people into repentance (a new way of thinking) were parables and miracles. Jesus' parables and miracles do not provide neat answers; more often than not they turn our world upside down and throw much into the rethink tank. This often involves learning how to ask better questions.

This chapter might better be titled "Why Wouldn't Everyone Ask Jesus To Get Out of Town?" C. S. Lewis wrote: "If you want a religion to make you feel really comfortable, I certainly don't recommend Christianity....I didn't go to religion to make me happy. I always knew a bottle of Port would do that."[9]   Responding to Jesus' "Follow me" will inevitably lead us out of our comfort zones. We will see things about ourselves and our world we have never seen before. We'll become aware of changes that should be made, things that ought to be done, and questions will surface we never thought of asking before. We will experience a reorientation of our thinking. This is the challenge Paul issues: *Let the same mind be in you that was in Christ Jesus* (Philippians 2:5); *Do not be conformed to this world but be transformed by the renewing of your minds....*(Romans 12:2). Isaiah 55:8-9 should be a daily reminder of the need for such renewal: *For my thoughts are not your thoughts, nor are your ways my ways, says the Lord. For as the heavens are higher than the earth, so are my ways higher than your ways and my thoughts than your thoughts.* In order to begin to understand the ways of God we have to change our way of thinking.

I don't want to conclude this chapter with the focus on the people who asked Jesus to get out of town. I want to conclude with the focus on the man whom those people found sitting (beside Jesus), dressed and in his right mind. If you were to ask him, "Are you glad Jesus came to your town?" there is no doubt as to his response. "Oh, yes! His visit changed my life!" And he would tell you his story. Mark's basic message might well be that what Jesus did so long ago he can do again – as long as we don't ask him to get out of town.

Reflections

Viewing the Bible as a "spectator" is not very troubling. When I begin to put myself into the role of the characters – and not just the good ones – I begin to come to some new and, often disturbing, insights. The people in the Mark 5 story had the situation under control or at least far enough away from them that they weren't bothered by it. When Jesus comes to town, he may have healed the demoniac but he disrupted the status quo. I can understand how upsetting Jesus' actions were. Perhaps the loss of livestock was secondary to the worry about what impact the former lunatic was going to have in the social context of their day.

We just don't like for things to go against the flow. "Don't upset the apple cart" is still the favorite mantra for many. It doesn't even matter if half the apples are rotten! "Peace at any price" has many applications and many levels. An in-depth exegesis of the text from Mark indicates that Jesus took the actions he did in order to bring about the restoration of the man. In the understanding of that day, the methods Jesus used were designed to demonstrate that this man was no longer possessed. Things may have been thrown into turmoil but no one could deny that here was a howling, unrestrained individual who was now seated, clothed, and in his right mind.

Am I willing to do what is necessary to bring about redemption, healing, and wholeness of mind and body to others? Am I willing to acknowledge that methods and ways I don't understand may be necessary? Am I willing to allow the status quo to be disrupted for the greater good? My confession is: too much of the time I am not!

[1]Philip Yancey, *What's So Amazing About Grace?* (Grand Rapids, Zondervan Publishing House, 1997), 153.

[2]John Andrew, *Nothing Cheap and Much That is Cheerful* (Grand Rapids, William B. Eerdmans Publishing Company, 1988), 5-6.

[3]Leonard Sweet, *Soul Tsunami* (Grand Rapids, Zondervan Publishing House, 1999), 99.

[4]*New International Version* (Grand Rapids, Zondervan Corporation, 1987).

[5]Mike Graves, *The Sermon as Symphony* (Valley Forge, Judson Press, 1997), 124.

[6]Jimmy Carter, *Living Faith* (New York, Times Books, 1996), 222.

[7]Dallas Willard, *The Divine Conspiracy* (New York, HarperSanFrancisco, 1998), 9-10.

[8]Ibid. 325.

[9]C. S. Lewis, *God in the Dock* (Grand Rapids, William B. Eerdman's Publishing Company, 1970), 58.

Chapter 10: Why Doesn't God Do What It Takes?

MODERN OBSERVATIONS:

The Serpent (in the Garden of Eden) seems to have discovered the one apparent weakness in God's armor, one limit to God's power, one seeming flaw in the design, and he immediately sets out to exploit it. He knows that the one thing the omnipotent God most desires – the free and loving response of the human heart – is something that cannot be secured by an exercise of power.[1]

The power that created the universe and spun the dragonfly's wing and is beyond all other powers holds back, in love, from overpowering us.[2]

There are two kinds of people: those who say to God, "Thy will be done," and those to whom God says, "All right, have it your way." C. S. Lewis.

"If only God would give me some clear sign; like a large deposit in my name at a Swiss bank." Woody Allen.

THE BIBLICAL TEXT: Matthew 11:20-24:

> *Then he began to reproach the cities in which most of his deeds of power had been done. "Woe to you, Chorazin! Woe to you, Bethsaida! For if the deeds of power done in you had been done in Tyre and Sidon, they would have repented long ago in sackcloth and ashes. But I tell you, on the day of judgment it will be more tolerable for Tyre and Sidon than for you. And you, Capernaum, will you be exalted to heaven? No, you will be brought down to Hades. For if the deeds of power done in you had been done in Sodom, it would have remained until this day. But I tell you that on the day of judgment it will be more tolerable for the land of Sodom than for you.*

One way of looking at this text is to conclude that

failure is a part of Jesus' ministry; the evangelistic campaigns he launches in three different cities are unsuccessful. (Mark 6:5-6 indicates the unbelief in Nazareth meant that Jesus *could do no deed of power there.*) Most have never heard of Chorazin and Bethsaida; Capernaum is remembered as Jesus' adopted hometown as an adult and the place of many of his healing miracles. To the surprise of three failures might also be added the surprise of the three woes Jesus pronounces on the cities. (For those nurtured on a "gentle Jesus, meek and mild," it might be profitable to check out how many times and to whom he says, "Woe to you!") The woes directed at the three cities are compounded by Jesus' announcement that on judgment day it will be more tolerable for Tyre, Sidon, and Sodom than these cities that witnessed his miracles. Tyre and Sidon are frequently denounced by Old Testament prophets and Sodom is notorious for its wickedness. Further adding to the confusion is Jesus' contention that if his deeds of power had been done in Tyre, Sidon, and Sodom, these cities would have repented. My question: if God knew what it would take for these cities to repent, why didn't he do it? Why doesn't God do what it takes?

From a text not frequently read and a question not frequently asked, in this chapter we will struggle with some matters that are at the heart of the Christian faith. In dealing with the question, "Why doesn't God do what it takes?" I will ask three other questions: (1) How far will God go? (2) What is God doing? (3) What is God after?

From the days of Saturday Roy Rogers and Gene Autry matinee movies with most little boys owning a cowboy outfit complete with holster and toy guns, comes the following story:

> *A grandfather proudly related his observation of a grandson playing preacher. The little lad, not knowing he was being watched, had decided to convene a church service while wearing a cowboy outfit. Standing behind his homemade pulpit, the young boy started to preach, choosing as his text the story of Jesus' raising Lazarus from the dead. As the make-believe preacher related to his imaginary congregation the sweep of this New Testament narrative, he dramatically quoted Jesus' command at the burial cave, "Lazarus, come out." After a brief period of silence, the young boy repeated the order. With still no movement in his simulated sanctuary, the grandson, lifted from his holsters two mock six-shooters and declared, "Alright, Lazarus, come out with your hands up."*[3]

Without a doubt, there are many times when God's exasperation far exceeds that of this young man. But, unlike this boy, God will not pull a gun on us, mock or otherwise. God always stops short of doing that which would take the decision out of our hands; God always stops short of making us an offer we can't refuse.

Centuries ago, St. Ambrose wrote: "What is impossible to God? Not that which is difficult to his power, but that which is contrary to his nature." God is not the godfather; he is the one we have come to know as the God and Father of our Lord and Savior Jesus Christ. In Jesus' life and ministry we most clearly see the one about whom the prophets wrote (Hebrews 11:1-3). Here is not a coercive, manipulative, overbearing tyrant but a God who sets limits on himself so as not to violate the humanity of the creatures he has made in his own image. In some tragic moments in church history there have been those who were willing to do whatever it took to force adherence to the faith as they interpreted it. They believed it was possible to "make" people Christians. They believed that whatever it took was what they ought to do.

My great disappointment in the church both then and now is that far too many proclaimed disciples are controlling, harsh, judgmental, and manipulative instead of being full of the fruit of the Spirit as described by Paul in Galatians 5:22: *The fruit of the Spirit is love, joy, peace, patience, kindness, generosity, faithfulness, gentleness, and self-control.* This is the nature of God and it ought to be the nature of God's people.

How far will God go? Revelation 3:20 reads: *Listen! I am standing at the door, knocking; if you hear my voice and open the door, I will come in to you and eat with you, and you with me.* (Although addressed to the church at Laodicea, this invitation has wide application: *Let anyone who has an ear listen to what the Spirit is saying to the churches* – Revelation 3:22.) God won't kick in the door. He won't demand that you come out with your hands up. God won't do anything that takes away your humanity, your dignity, your right to say yes or no.

Charlie Brown once observed: "I never do anything right. If life were a camera, I'd have the lens cap on." Charlie Brown has no monopoly on the lens-cap mentality. It was a disability for many of those in ancient Chorazin, Bethsaida, and Capernaum. They couldn't see what God was doing in their midst. It is a great mistake to read the miracles in the Bible as signs nobody could miss. Many did. When Jesus performs his deeds of power, some believe and some don't. It is never as clear-cut as we would like to make

115

it; it is never so obvious that there cannot be doubt. (I have never heard a sermon on Matthew 18:16-17: *Now, the eleven disciples went to Galilee, to the mountain to which Jesus had directed them. When they saw him, they worshipped him; but some doubted.*) One author questions: "How many times in the wilderness did Moses wonder if the burning bush had just been desert heatstroke?"[4]

Jesus was busy doing God's deeds of power in the cities that chose not to respond. But they didn't view them as God's deeds of power; they didn't hear Jesus' words as Spirit-filled words. They had the same option we all have: "God will not hurl pronouncements from the sky such that people must listen. As is evident in the history of the world, a characteristic of God is that God grants us the option to ignore."[5] Jesus often said, *"Blessed are those who have eyes to see and ears to hear."* In other words, "Blessed are those who do not have the lens cap on life's camera. Blessed are those who are not blind to what God is doing in the world. Blessed are those who are able to hear God's *gentle whisper*" (I Kings 19:12; NIV). The noisy, cluttered, showmanship world continues to make it difficult to perceive spiritual realities. Too many believe that what God does is always spectacular enough to knock your socks off; it is on such a grand scale that you can't miss it. Chorazin, Bethsaida, and Capernaum all missed what Jesus terms his *deeds of power.*

A popular book on spirituality has a reflection applicable to the Christian faith:

> *The various practices known as prayer, meditation, contemplation, and yoga have been highly valued over the centuries because they sharpen attention and make it easier not to miss the clues to spirituality. A spiritual*

person is a good listener for silent voices, a sharp observer of invisible objects.[6]

What is God doing? Only those who have eyes to see and ears to hear even begin to understand.

In one of the *Kudzu* comic strips, Doris, the parrot, is on her perch looking toward the window. She is thinking: "The window is open. I've got to decide, do I stay and lead a life of security at the price of boredom? Or do I fly and risk the adventure of fending for myself, never knowing where my next meal is coming from? All I have to do is fly over the windowsill – the choice is mine! FOR GOSH SAKES, WOULD SOMEBODY PLEASE SHUT THAT WINDOW!"

Because of what God is after, he will always leave the window open, just as he did in the Garden of Eden. He didn't place an electric fence around the forbidden tree; it was right out there in the open, for the taking. Why? Because God was after relationship freely chosen, the loving relationship of the Creator with those whom he had created in his own image.

The Parable of the Prodigal Son (not the preferred designation as will be discussed in Chapter 12) is the story of a father who leaves the window open. It is the story of a father who permits his younger son to journey to a distant country and *squander his wealth in wild living* (Luke 15:13; NIV). It is the story of a father who keeps watching, and hoping, and praying that his son will decide to come back home. When the son finally returns there is joy and celebration that would have been impossible without the son's freedom to go and freedom to return. Love, forgiveness, and reconciliation make the relationship between father and son everything it was meant to be.

Louis Evely succinctly stated the truth: "If God saved by force all (people) and imposed his presence upon them, heaven would be nothing more than a huge concentration camp." The biblical story hardly gets underway before God comes searching and calling, "Adam, where are you?" He doesn't shout, "Come out with your hands up!" The Bible is the incredible story of God who loves and woos and seeks his wandering and stubborn creatures. Its climax is the account of the God who loves his world so much that he gives his only begotten son. The cross is God's mightiest deed of power. It is the power of love, the power God uses to bring us to himself because only love can summon the response of love. *(We love because he first loved us* – I John 4:19). The cross is God's supreme and ultimate offer of forgiveness and reconciliation. Jesus said, *"And I, when I am lifted up from the earth, will draw all people to myself* (John 12:32). Commenting on this verse, a minister writes:

> *The Master...trusted his cause to the power of persuasion.... Whatever consequence was to come from his ministry could come only from the appeal of his life and love and sacrifice, drawing to himself (people's) voluntary allegiance. The amazing thing is that he trusted in that.*[7]

He trusted in that because he knew what it takes to accomplish what God is after.

Reflections

A woman once asked Bertrand Russell, a well-known atheist, what he would say if it turned out he had been wrong and found himself standing outside the Pearly Gates. His eyes lighting up, Russell replied in his high, thin voice, "Why, I should say, "God, you gave us insufficient evidence!"[8] Russell never said what kind of evidence it would take to be "sufficient." I admit I do not understand the mind of an atheist. Belief in God has always been a part of my life and my doubts have not been about God's existence. I do not doubt Russell's sincerity and I have not read enough about his life to know what helped to shape his mind-set.

This quote is not only about prayer but about revelation in general: "Prayer is primarily attentiveness to God's disclosure to us and the heart's response to that disclosure."[9] Paul asserts in Romans 1 that there is ample evidence in the creation itself for belief in God's existence. Not everybody would agree with that thesis. For those of us who are believers, we marvel at the world around us, the expanse above us, and the incredible microscopic and sub-microscopic world beyond our apprehension. The complexity, diversity, and expansiveness of life are enough for us to believe in a divine creator.

I wish I could have asked Russell if he wanted evidence that took away his right to believe or not believe. Did he want God to be so overwhelming that he had no choice in the matter? The totality of the biblical witness (there is that phrase again) indicates for me that God has always been one who invites, woos, seeks, implores, and builds bridges. (More about this in Chapter 11.) If what

God is after is a relationship of loving-trust, I don't see how it can come any other way. If we can't really say "No" then we can never really say "Yes."

I worry that those who want irrefutable evidence cannot see the danger of our becoming robots instead of the human beings created in his image that God intends for us to be.

[1]William Frey, *The Dance of Hope* (Colorado Springs, Waterbrook Press, 2003), 26.

[2]Frederick Buechner, *Telling Secrets* (New York, HarperSanFrancisco, 1991), 28.

[3]Thomas David Austin, *Faith Journey of a Pilgrim* (Macon, Symth & Helwys, 2000), 19.

[4]Daniel Taylor, *The Myth of Christianity* (Waco, Jarrell, 1986), 9.

[5]David J. Wolpe, *In Speech and In Silence* (New York, Henry Holt and Company, 1992), 153.

[6]Deepak Chopra, *How To Know God* (New York, Harmony Books, 2000), 196.

[7]Harry Emerson Fosdick, *A Great Time To Be Alive* (New York, Harper & Brothers, 1944), 163.

[8]Philip Yancey, *Reaching for the Invisible God*, 35.

[9]Martin Smith, *The Word Is Very Near You* (Cambridge, Cowley Publications, 1989), 19.

Chapter 11: God's Surprising Strategy

MODERN OBSERVATIONS:

Apologetics must always look like God's love at work.[1]

What is remarkable is not how many bad things happen to good people but how many good things happen to bad people.[2]

We teach that God is unconditional love and seldom, in fact never, take that seriously enough. Our generation likes to believe that we have freed ourselves from some older fears. God was sometimes seen as someone with a big stick, ready to punish us for every weakness and infidelity, or as someone with a big book, recording every one of our sins in view of some great future reckoning. We have moved a bit beyond this, though not nearly as much as we give ourselves credit for....In conservative circles, God is hung-up on orthodoxy, of dogma and morals. In liberal circles, God is hung-up on social justice. In neither circle is he very joyous, understanding, and compassionate. We are still a long way from appropriating that God was incarnate in Jesus. Do we ever really take the unconditional love of God seriously?[3]

THE BIBLICAL TEXT: Romans 2:1-4:

Therefore you have no excuse, whoever you are, when you judge others; for in passing judgment on another you condemn yourself, because you, the judge, are doing the same things. You say, "We know that God's judgment on those who do such things is in accordance with the truth." Do you imagine, whoever you are, that when you judge those who do such things and yet do them yourself, you will escape the judgment of God? Or do you despise the

riches of his kindness and forbearance and patience? Do
you not realize that God's kindness is meant to lead you
to repentance?

William Archibald Spooner (1844-1930) is the patron
saint of all of us who remember embarrassing tongue-
tangled pulpit moments. Spooner frequently reversed the
initial letters or syllables of two or more words in his
Anglican sermons. "A crushing blow" became "a blushing
crow" and "I have a half-formed wish in my mind" became
"I have a half-warmed fish in my mind." These slips of the
tongue came to be known as "spoonerisms." Others
include: "foon and spork" (spoon and fork); "when your
tumb gets nongue" (tongue gets numb); and "you didn't
hear a thingle sing I said" (single thing). In a sermon
emphasizing how "The Lord is a loving Shepherd," the
congregation was informed that "The Lord is a shoving
leopard."[4] This was not what the minister believed or
intended to say but I suspect his malapropism is closer to
the beliefs of many than they would like to confess.

If Satan prowls about like a roaring lion (I Peter 5:8),
then perhaps God might be more effective as a shoving
leopard. In a slip of the tongue, Spooner gave expression to
an undisclosed conviction of some about the way God
ought to work in persuading persons to follow him and do
his will. It's the old "You can get more with a kind word
and a gun than you can with just a kind word" philosophy.
Surely people would pay more attention to an aggressive
shoving leopard than to an apparently rather passive loving
shepherd. In Romans 2:1-4, Paul says something about
God's strategy that is not a slip of the tongue. (Remember,
as Romans 16:22 tells us, Paul did not write this, he dictated

it to Tertius.) Even though to many it may sound like a spoonerism, I assure you it is not. It is God's surprising strategy.

The misunderstanding and the surprise were inherent in the beginning: *Do you despise the riches of his kindness and forbearance and patience? Do you not realize that God's kindness is meant to lead you to repentance?* The Greek construction indicates that Paul is telling them, "Yes, you do! You despise (take lightly, fail to give due weight to) God's kindness, forbearance, and patience." It appears that those to whom Paul was writing despised God's kindness because there were convinced they were special and exempt from the kind of judgment that would fall on the Gentiles whose sins Paul enumerates in Romans 1. Paul quickly reminds them that *God shows no partiality* (2:11) when it comes to judgment (holding us accountable). He underscores a major tenant of scripture: we are the judged and not the judges. The initial hearers of this letter (this is the way most people in the world of that day would have received it) were not far from trading on the goodness of God, not realizing that God's kindness is his great strategy to lead them to repentance.

It is just as easy to despise God's goodness for a different reason: the belief that it doesn't "work." Kindness, forbearance, and patience are viewed as "being soft on sin" and not efficacious for producing genuine repentance; *God's kindness is meant to lead you to repentance* cannot be taken at face value. Several years ago, a writer reported that every time he ran the spell-check program on his word processor, it wanted to change to word "sacred" to "scared."[5] The programmer of that spell-check probably never meant to equate sacred with scared, even though it is all too frequently assumed that if God is going to get people to change he is going to have to scare the wits (or whatever) out of them. I don't see how this correlates with the keystone of God's saving strategy: *For God so loved the world that he gave his only Son* (John 3:16).

Some boys and girls in a Sunday School class were listening intently to the lesson for the morning about the crucifixion. One youngster was literally on the edge of his chair as the teacher told how Jesus was nailed to the cross. Before the teacher could finish, the boy blurted out, "I bet if Superman had been there they wouldn't have gotten away with it!"[6] I'm certain the rest of the story conveys that no one "got away" with anything. Jesus says, *"I lay down my life for the sheep....No one takes it from me, but I lay it down of my own accord"* (John 10:15, 18). God's intentional strategy of this magnitude of sacrificial love is beyond comprehension. Paul has to pile up phrases to even begin to describe the treasures of God's goodness: *the riches of his kindness* literally means *the wealth of his kindness.* And when things are so bad that you can't imagine how they could get any worse (the description of the human predicament in the beginning of Romans), Paul writes that God brings out his ultimate weapon: *Where sin abounded, God's grace super-abounded* (Romans 5:20).

The strategy of grace, kindness, and love is consistent with the central images in the Bible about how God seeks to win us over. Revelation 3:20: *I am standing at the door, knocking; if you hear my voice and open the door, I will come in and eat with you, and you with me.* "Christ still stands at the door and knocks. It is a gentle knocking....He does not pick the lock, much less break down the door."[7] There is no shoving leopard pawing at the door; there is a loving shepherd gently knocking. For many, the biggest surprise of all in God's strategy is that, in the light of his purposes (leading us to repentance), it does work.

Lucy and Linus are watching TV. Lucy asks, "Why don't you get me a dish of ice cream?" Linus responds, "What would you do if I told you to get it yourself?" Lucy tells him, "I'd pound you until the sun went down, and I'd keep on pounding you until the sun came up and then I'd pound you until the sun went down again." Linus asks: "Chocolate or vanilla?" Lucy has a strategy that works – for getting ice cream. But if she wants a good relationship with her brother, it doesn't work. If all God wants from us is certain behavior, I have no doubt he could readily force compliance. The *repentance* that is meant to be the response to God's kindness, forbearance, and patience is far more than modified behavior. The New Testament word translated "repentance" is *metanoia;* it means a change of mind, a change of attitude, a change of direction. This is a complete reorientation of life that is rooted in a new relationship with God. I John 4:18-19: *There is no fear in love, but perfect love casts out fear; for fear has to do with punishment, and whoever fears has not reached perfection in love. We love because he first loved us.*

God's strategy is the perfect strategy for the kind of change and growth involved in being the kind of person God intends us to be – the kind of person who reflects being created in his image. The atmosphere of wrath and punishment produces a different kind of person. The motivation of fear is not conducive for producing persons who look like the kingdom citizens described in the Sermon on the Mount (Matthew 5 – 7). Paul states God's ultimate purpose for all of us in Romans 8:28-29:

> *We know that in all things God works for the good of those who love him, who have been called according to his purpose. For those God foreknew he also predestined to be conformed to the likeness of his Son, that he might be the firstborn with a large family.*

God's goal in repentance *(metanoia)* is that we become increasingly like his model for humanity, Jesus Christ. In our attitudes, philosophies, goals, ambitions, and relationships we are to seek the pattern in Jesus' teaching and ministry. How is this achieved? Can you imagine Jesus telling his disciples: "You'd better do what God says or he'll beat the tar out of you. The only reason I do what he says is because I'm afraid not to. I've warned you repeatedly and you haven't taken me seriously. Either do it now or God will whip you into shape by methods I don't even want to think about." Such speculation is impossible in the life and ministry of the one who felt so incredibly loved by the Father that every day of his life was one of joyful obedience of a loving son to a loving father. *"My food is to do the will of him who sent me and to complete his work"* (John 4:34).

We know what Jesus does say (John 15:9-12):

> *As the Father has loved me, so have I loved you. Now remain in my love. If you obey my commands, you will remain in my love, just as I have obeyed my Father's commands and remain in his love. I have told you this so that my joy may be in you and that your joy may be complete. My command is this: Love one another as I have loved you.*

The fulfilling of commands is always in the context of love. The central commandment (which summarizes the entire

Law) has to do with loving God with heart, mind, soul, and strength and our neighbors as ourselves. Jesus' command (often termed The Eleventh Commandment) establishes the priority of living out the divine/human relationships under the rubric of the kind of love demonstrated in Jesus' life and ministry.

In the New Testament salvation is all of grace and ethics is the response of gratitude. An unfortunate arrangement of material has taken the punch out of what I consider Paul's greatest *"therefore."* Romans 12:1 begins with this word and it only makes sense when read after chapter eight. In that mountain peak chapter, Paul writes about *no condemnation for those of us in Christ Jesus; the Spirit who raised Jesus from the dead dwelling in us; our being led by the Spirit of God who bears witness with our spirits that we are children of God; the sufferings of this present time are not worth comparing with the glory that will be revealed to us; the Spirit interceding for us in our weakness when we don't even have words for our prayers; God cooperating with us in everything for good; since God is for us, no one (or anything) can ever effectively be against us; nothing can ever separate us from God's love in Jesus Christ.... THEREFORE:*

> *I appeal to you, brothers and sisters, by the mercies of God, to present your bodies as a living sacrifice, holy and acceptable to God, which is your spiritual worship. Do not be conformed to this world, but be transformed by the renewing of your minds, so that you may discern what is the will of God – what is good and acceptable and perfect.* (Romans 12:1-2).

In its context, the above passage is the logical response of those who find themselves overwhelmed by God's grace.

Using a line from the gospel hymn "Just As I Am," a writer, whose name and source have long been forgotten, made this profound statement:

> *God is all-wise. He knows that the batterings of force only harden and stiffen, while the appeals to mercy and love break down the hardest wills and creates the most lasting commitments. "Just as I am, thy love unknown has broken every barrier down." And so it does. And so throughout the Bible those tender, loving appeals ring out from a God who could easily blast his way to success. Thank you, Lord, for respecting me enough to win me by love and not by force!*

This has always been God's strategy both in the Old Testament under the First Covenant and in the New Testament under the New Covenant. We have already noted the more accurate translation from Psalm 23: *Surely goodness and mercy shall pursue me all the days of my life.* To accomplish his purposes for all his creation, this is God's strategy. He doesn't have a backup plan. There is no plan B in which God breaks down doors and makes offers you can't refuse. His surprising strategy is his only strategy. If we don't respond to his offer of love, grace, mercy, and forgiveness, he has nothing else to give.

Reflections

If one is not careful, reading through the Old Testament might lead one to believe that God's strategy was to terrorize people into submission. If people didn't do what God asked (mainly – worshiped only him), he had a set of woes that ought to make anybody think twice. But a careful reading of the Old Testament reveals that even the

God of the First Covenant did not use punishment as his strategy for obedience. Even with this covenant his goal was relationship with his people. I believe Yancey is correct when he writes: "In fact, it was God's compassion, not power, that first impressed the Hebrews."[8]   The Old Testament is full of passages that speak of God's compassion, mercy, forgiveness, and love.

My biggest argument for believing that God's strategy in the Old Testament is the same as in the New Testament is because of the strategy Jesus demonstrated in his life and ministry. I recommend Philip Yancey's *The Bible Jesus Read* as the great reminder of this often ignored fact and for a more positive take on the contents of the Hebrew Bible. The Church early declared that it was heresy to teach that the God of the Old Testament was different from the God of the New Testament. (Marcion completley rejected the Old Testament.)   Without discounting the difficulties encountered in some sections of the Old Testament, the bigger story is the one Jesus brought in his teaching and ministry out of his interpretation of his Bible.

There has been much written about the healing power of unconditional love. Most of the major changes in my life (even if they come slowly) come as the result of being graced and loved unconditionally. Years ago, I preached a sermon titled "What Really Changes People?" based on the story of Jesus' encounter with Zacchaeus (Luke 19:1-10). When Jesus invites himself to be a luncheon guest of a notorious tax-collector (who is literally up a tree and out on a limb), the religious community is outraged. Whatever Zacchaeus already knew about Jesus, we are not told. We are told of the impact Jesus' offer makes on him: *"I will give half my wealth to the poor, Lord, and if I have overcharged people on their taxes, I will give them back four times as much"* (Luke 19:8).

This response did not come about as a result of a lecture by Jesus on the evils of the Roman tax system and the corruption involved. Condemnation is not a liberating word, grace is. Grace offers possibilities that condemnation never offers. "You rotten no good sinner," is not very therapeutic. This was NEVER the technique Jesus uses with sinners. Grace is the word that invites people to change. My questions are: Did those who murmured and grumbled that day help Zacchaeus? Did their condemnation, even though true and just deserved, produce a change in his life?

[1]John G. Stackhouse, Jr., *Humble Apologetics* (Oxford University Press, 2002), 141.

[2]Louis Evely, *We Dare To Say Our Father* (New York, Herder and Herder, 1989), 86.

[3]Ronald Rolheiser, *Against an Infinite Horizon* (New York, Crossroad Publishing Company, 1992), 136.

[4]*Homiletics,* Volume 9, Number 2, April-June 1997, 13.

[5]*Homiletics,* Volume 9, Number 1, January-March 1997, 35.

[6]Dick Van Dyke, *Faith, Hope and Hilarity* (Garden City, Doubleday and Company, 1970), 30.

[7]George Arthur Buttrick, *God, Pain, and Evil* (Nashville, Abingdon Press, 1966), 132.

[8]Philip Yancey, *Reaching for the Invisible God,* 130.

Chapter 12: Upsetting Grace

MODERN OBSERVATIONS:
...when the Bible pictures God's future world, there's always a party.[1]

We have heard this story (of the prodigal son) so often that we are no longer amazed by its wild extravagance, its incredible mercy.[2]

We are such bookkeepers! And God is not! When the Ninevites repent (in the story of Jonah), and the ne'er-do-wells at the end of the line get paid the same as the hard workers at the front of the line, and the people we judge most harshly receive the mercy of God, then it becomes painfully clear that there is something inherently unfair in the notion of grace. God does not keep track of things the way we do. God does not spend a lot of time deciding who is worthy and who is not, like we do.[3]

THE BIBLICAL TEXT: Luke 15:25-32:

> *Now his elder son was in the field; and when he came and approached the house, he heard music and dancing. He called one of the slaves and asked what was going on. He replied, "Your brother has come, and your father has killed the fatted calf, because he has got him back safe and sound." Then he became angry and refused to go in. His father came out and began to plead with him. But he answered his father, "Listen! For all these years I have been working like a slave for you, and I have never disobeyed your command; yet you have never given me even a young goat so that I might celebrate with my friends. But when this son of yours came back, who has devoured your property with prostitutes, you killed the fatted calf for him!" Then the father said to him, "Son, you are always with me, and all that is mine is yours. But we had to celebrate and rejoice, because this brother of yours was dead and has come to life; he was lost and*

has been found.

This is no doubt Jesus' most famous parable; its familiarity has probably bred something far worse than contempt. Fred Craddock suggests that when a minister reads a familiar passage of scripture on which the forthcoming sermon is to be based, you can almost hear the congregation saying, "Well, here we go again." Craddock contends that what is nearer the truth is that most of them have never been the first time. This parable has been so dissected, analyzed, and explained (always the death knell for a parable) that it has lost its wallop. Jesus' parables are meant to knock our socks off, take away our breath. My contention is that if we read this parable and don't experience a jolt of some kind, we have very likely sailed right over it.

The shock value of this story is discovered only in its context that requires the reading of all of chapter 15 in Luke. This is not an isolated story; it is part of a trilogy Jesus tells in response to grumbling from some in the faith community about Jesus' welcoming and eating with sinners. The first story is about a man who has a hundred sheep, loses one, finds it, then throws a party and invites his friends to come and rejoice with him. They come. The second story is about a woman who has ten coins (perhaps her dowry), loses one, finds it, then throws a party and invites her friends to come and rejoice with her. They come. The third story is about a man who has two sons, loses one, finds him, then throws a party and invites his friends to come and rejoice with him. All of the invited guests come except for the older son who refuses to attend. Jesus sets the grumbling of the scribes and Pharisees and the anger of the elder brother over against the celebration that concludes each story. Why the grumbling? Why the anger? The answer (then and now) is: upsetting grace.

The "problem" of upsetting grace is a continuing disconcertion in Jesus' ministry. In Matthew 20, Jesus compares the kingdom of heaven with a landowner who goes to the local labor exchange and hires workers to harvest his crop. The periodic hirings occur at 6:00 a.m., 9:00 a.m., noon, 3:00 p.m., and 5:00 p.m. Daily workers were paid at the end of the day; the line forms at 6:00 p.m. with those who worked only one hour at the front. All receive a full day's pay for their work. Those who labored all day grumble (the same grumbling we find in Luke 15:1) that the rate for one hour is the same as for twelve hours! The story concludes with this question from the owner of the vineyard: *"Are you envious because I am so generous?"* The unvoiced response is, "You bet we are!" The compensation for the last hired is totally out of proportion to what is deserved. But this is not a story about wage disputes; it is a kingdom parable. The story is about God's uncalculating generosity, God's immeasurable compassion.

Ephesians 2:8-9: *For by grace you have been saved through faith, and this is not your own doing; it is the gift of God – not of works, so that no one may boast.* Entirely too many have a reasonable gospel for reasonable people in a reasonable world. All three phrases are biblical oxymorons. The Bible espouses an unreasonable gospel for unreasonable people in an unreasonable world. It's all about grace called amazing because it is unreasonable. It is unreasonable that a young man who disgraces himself and his father, throws away his inheritance, and comes home with the lingering aroma of the pig sty, can be welcomed into his father's house with the biggest party the community has ever seen. The Pharisees, the scribes, the elder brother, and many of us dutiful religious folk still get bent out of shape over the offense of grace. It is so unreasonable but absolutely necessary. It means you can never out-sin God's grace, you can never out-distance God's love. You can never find yourself in a pit so deep but that God's mercy is deeper still. God's superabundant extravagances were always there, but began to be appropriated the moment of the younger son's receptivity: *But when he came to himself he said, "I will get up and go to my Father, and I will say to him, "Father, I have sinned...."*

As the son makes his way back home, he never struggles with the question of mercy or merit. The second part of his rehearsed speech reveals that he already knows the answer to that one: *"I am no longer worthy to be called your son."* This is placed in sharp contrast to his elder brother who in essence tells his father: *"For all these years I have been working like a slave for you. Where's my party? Unlike this no account son of yours, I deserve one!"* He is full of anger (according to the text, literally "rage") because of the unfairness of the situation. After all, he is entitled (the most dangerous and deadly tag a Christian can appropriate!).

I am usually able to upset a considerable number of listeners whenever I teach that the only people who are going to be in heaven are those who know they don't deserve to be there. What would heaven be like if it were only for the entitled! It would be like an eternal "Bragging 101" college course. I believe the old Gomer Pyle mantra will be the one those gathered will repeat throughout eternity: "Thank you! Thank you! Thank you!" A heaven filled with gratitude will be truly heaven. What other response could one possibly make? *He who did not withhold his own Son, but GAVE him up for all of us, will he not with him also GIVE us everything else?* (Romans 8:32). I insist that you really come to yourself when you finally discover that everything is gift. Everything is grace. We are not on God's payroll; we're on his gift list. This means there is no limit to what we can receive.

Calling the story "The Parable of the Prodigal Son" (which neither Jesus or Luke ever announce as a title), easily leads one to miss the intended focus. The focus of the story is neither of the two sons; the story is about the father. Ann Lamott's *Traveling Mercies* is a marvelous and provocative book. One of her many unsettling lines is: "I wish I'd been given a mother who liked children."[4] The story Jesus tells is about a father who loves his sons. The real tragedy is that the elder brother does not know how much he is loved.

This is not a story about a first-century dad. This is the story about the God of Abraham, Isaac, and Jacob; the God and Father of our Lord and Savior Jesus Christ. It is the story of the God who truly, genuinely, and eternally loves all of us. Jesus is the friend of sinners because God is the friend of sinners. Jesus comes to seek and save the lost because that's the business God is in (ever since the Garden of Eden). Jesus never meets anyone who is outside the circle of his love because God never draws a circle of exclusion. This parable has been appropriately called "The Parable of the Waiting Father," but I prefer another title.

As the younger son begins his journey home, we are told that the father sees him while he is still a long way off. In spite of the social indignity, the father runs to meet him. My favorite title for this story is "The Parable of the Running Father." I'm convinced the father kept his running shoes on all the time the younger son was gone; he was ready to sprint into action the moment he spotted him in the distance. Here is the picture of the Heavenly Father.

Running to meet us with the stench of the pig pen still on us. Running to meet us no matter how far away our far country has been. Running to meet us because we have never been out of his love. Running to meet us because he has already forgiven us and is simply waiting for us to receive it.

You will notice that the younger son doesn't get all the way through his rehearsed speech. "The prodigal's father doesn't wait to hear another word about the whole episode. He gives a banquet. That's how God does it too. He alone can make forgiveness something glorious to remember."[5] The extent of the celebration is hinted at when the elder brother hears music from inside the house. The word for music is our word for symphony. When the younger son comes home and the father throws a party, he doesn't bring in a lyre and flute duo; he hires the entire Jerusalem Philharmonic Orchestra!

As with many of Jesus' parables, this story leaves us hanging. Because the elder son is so angry that his undeserving brother has been given such a welcome home party, he refuses to go in and join the festivities. We are told that *his father came out and began to plead with him.* Literally: *he kept on beseeching him.* That's how the story ends. It is an open-ended story with questions to be answered and decisions to be made. Will we share in the celebration in the Father's house? Will we share in God's mercy? Will we share in God's grace and love for all? Will we be as inclusive as God is? Will we be able to rejoice in God's generosity?

Years ago, I remember visiting in a nursing home with a man who was critically ill. We had known each other a long time and I knew he had deep regrets about some of the things in his life. In the course of our conversation, he paused, and, with a rather grim expression, asked, "Do you think I will go to heaven?" I returned, "Do you think I will go to heaven?" Without a moment's hesitation, he said, "Oh, yes." "Why do you think that?" He thought for awhile, smiled, and said, "Well, I've heard enough of your sermons to know the answer: only by God's grace." "That's right," I agreed, and he gave me an even bigger smile. That was the last conversation I ever had with him; I conducted his funeral service shortly thereafter. I have thought often about that final discussion and the broad smile with which it concluded. I am convinced the smile on his face that day was nothing compared to the smile he must have had when he heard the words we all finally long to hear: "Welcome home." What I fully believe is: if it weren't for upsetting grace, none of us would ever hear it.

Reflections

I wish I didn't believe the truth of these words. Unfortunately, I know by experience that they are true:

> *The Church has always been afraid of being as loving as its Master. We just cannot really believe that "this man receives sinners." Still less can we really believe that he is the "friend of sinners," and, on his own word, loves them as much as he loves the saints.*[6]

I once heard a sermon on my car radio in which the minister asked, "What did Jesus do that so upset people?" He paused and then said, "He preached against sin!" I almost ran off the road! Whatever else you may find about Jesus' conflicts in the gospels, you will not find this. First of all, it was the religious establishment that was so upset with him. The sinners welcomed him with open arms – just as he welcomed them. And that was the problem! Jesus never drew a circle that left anyone out of God's love and acceptance. He was never afraid that someone would believe that, in welcoming sinners, he was endorsing sin.

I have always found it difficult to "hate the sin but love the sinner." Whenever there is hate, I find it difficult to keep it in check. (Also, I don't believe that oft heard phrase is a verse of scripture.) Jesus saw as his mission the seeking and saving (bringing about restoration, wholeness, etc.) to those who were lost. He just never seemed to be bothered by those who railed against his inclusion of outcasts, "known sinners," Samaritans, and Gentiles in his definition of the Kingdom of God.

All I know is: God's grace has never upset me. It continues to be my only hope.

[1]David Buttrick, *Preaching the New and the Now*, 127.
[2]Morton Kelsey, *Afterlife* (New York, Crossroad Publishing Company, 1982), 177.
[3]Barbara Brown Taylor, *Gospel Medicine* (Boston, Crowley Publications, 1995), 93.
[4]Anne Lamott, *Traveling Mercies*, 83.
[5]Louis Evely, *That Man Is You* (New York, The Newman Press, 1966), 137.
[6]Leslie Weatherhead, *Time for God* (Nashville, Abingdon, 1967), 37.

Part III: From Fear to Faith in God's Ways

Points to Ponder

In a careful reading of Mark 5, we may discover that we are just as disturbed by what Jesus does as the anonymous townsfolk are.

"Peace! Be still!" is most often heard only after we have been battered by a terrible storm of hurricane proportions.

Jesus' parables and miracles do not provide neat answers; more often than not they turn our world upside down and throw much into the rethink tank.

God always stops short of making us an offer we can't refuse.

Too many believe that what God does is always spectacular enough to knock your socks off; it is on such a grand scale that you can't miss it.

The cross is God's mightiest deed of power. It is the power of love, the power God uses to bring us to himself because only love can elicit the response of love.

If Satan prowls around like a roaring lion (I Peter 5:8), would God be more effective as a shoving leopard?

The strategy of grace, kindness, and love is consistent with the central images in the Bible about how God seeks to win us over.

In the New Testament salvation is of grace and ethics is the response of gratitude.

Entirely too many have a reasonable gospel for reasonable people in a reasonable world. All three phrases are biblical oxymorons.

What would heaven be like if it were only for the entitled?

How about this as the title for the famous parable in Luke 15: "The Parable of the Running Father."

Part IV: From Fear to Faith in Eternal Matters

Chapter 13: If Jesus Didn't Know the Date for the End of the World, Does Anyone Else?

MODERN OBSERVATIONS:

The problem lies in our trying to pin down chronologically and literalistically events that are part of the cyclic symbolism of multi-layered mystery of (the book of) Revelation.[1]

This survey of Western end-time thinking is intended to demonstrate two themes – doomsday ideas have been both persistent and adaptable......Through two thousand years of Western history millions of people have believed they were living in the last days.[2]

While apocalyptic millennialism was strong in the early church, on the whole the early church fathers shied away from specific date-setting.[3]

THE BIBLICAL TEXT: Mark 13:7-8, 32-37:

> *"When you hear of wars and rumors of wars, do not be alarmed; this must take place, but the end is still to come. For nation will rise against nation, and kingdom against kingdom; there will be earthquakes in various places; there will be famines. This is but the beginnings of the birthpangs.*

"But about that day or hour no one knows, neither the angels in heaven, nor the Son, but only the Father. Beware, keep alert; for you do not know when the time will come. It is like a man going on a journey, when he leaves home, and puts his slaves in charge, each with his work, and commands the doorkeeper to be on the watch. Therefore, keep awake – for you do not know when the master of the house will come, in the evening, or at midnight, or at cockcrow, or at the dawn, or else he may find you asleep when he comes suddenly. And what I say to you I say to all: Keep awake."

It's a question that won't go away. I don't know who first asked it but I know who asked it about 2,000 years ago. Mark 13:3-4 informs us that Peter, James, John, and Andrew get Jesus off in a corner and ask, *"Tell us, when will this be, and what will be the sign that all these things are about to be accomplished."* They have just exited the Temple compound and commented to Jesus on the impressive buildings and the massive stones. Jesus remarks that one day all of this will be heaps of rubble. The disciples are stunned; the inner four invite Jesus to a caucus and want to know when this will happen and what sign they need to watch for indicating this destruction is about to occur. Their private question to Jesus has become the most public question in the religious world. Their preoccupation with dates and signs has become the chief occupation of many of Jesus' followers. What was once discussed in a huddle is now printed and telecast and lectured on *ad infinitum*.

The disciples are not rebuffed for asking their question about the coming destruction of the Temple; Jesus tells them that the signs are many and the time is soon. Israel is on a collision course with Rome and in 70 A.D. the heap of rubble prediction is fulfilled. Mark 13 not only speaks about the destruction of Jerusalem but also about the coming of the Son of Man in power and glory, or what most currently term the Second Coming of Christ and the "end of the world." (Matthew 28:20 is translated in the King James: *I am with you always, even unto the end of the world.* The better, and I believe correct, translation is: *...to the end of the age.*) In answering the question, it is important to note that Jesus gives a two-event answer. He does two other things with the question. First, he redirects the question (as we will soon see); second, he says something his disciples thought they would never hear him say, "I don't know." *But about that day or hour no one knows, neither the angels in heaven, nor the Son, but only the Father.* In the light of this verse it may appear redundant to ask, "If Jesus didn't know the date for the end of the world (age), does anyone else?"but the current apocalyptic deluge makes it imperative.

Beginning shortly before the new millennium, there began what many call the biggest "doom boom" in the history of the world. Since the Middle Ages the doomers have been booming, but this doom boom is different. Up until now the end of the world stuff was on the edges of society. It looked strange and out of place. Today the "apparatus of modern communications – cable television, video recordings, and mass market paperbacks – has brought apocalyptic themes from the theological and social margins...into the main stream of American awareness.[3]

Several years ago, I purchased a book titled "Wow! The Apocalypse Now!" The first page contains this box: "Before the World Ended, This Book Belonged To _____." It is filled with fascinating past and present apocalyptic ideas and   a highly irreverent "Doomsday Final Exam" where you can test your End-Times IQ. I found the book to be much needed comic relief to the obsession about end times. Jesus did not dwell on the subject, Paul warned some of his readers who had become fixated on it, and church history shows that those for whom the Doom Boom was the only boom in town, did themselves, and usually everyone else, a great disservice. While the Bible plainly teaches the return of our Lord and the final consummation of history, there is no place that even hints this should become the major focus in the life of the believer.

There are some things you should know about the end of the world (age). From the earliest New Testament times, believers have felt that the end was near. Those who lived in Paul's day expected the imminent return of Christ. There has never been a time since then when people believed any sign had to be fulfilled before the Lord could return. For them the signs were everywhere and were everywhere fulfilled. When Jesus speaks about war, earthquakes, and famines, he is speaking about present occurrences in his day. (The most deadly earthquake took place in central China in 1556 when approximately 830,000 people perished.)[4]

What is new in our time is the dispensational premillennialism that has swept through the evangelical world in popular books and novels. Many believe this is the clear teaching of scripture, but it is only one way to read the scripture and many are convinced it is not the best way. This interpretation took off due to the influence of the Scofield Reference Bible, first published in 1909. Rather than end notes or a separate commentary, this Bible includes center notes and footnotes that many view as almost as inspired as the text of Holy Scripture. Scoffield places the creation of the world at 4004 B.C. (after Archbishop Usshur) and divides human history into seven dispensations (after John Nelson Darby). According to this scheme of things we are living in the "church age." I argue that, biblically, there is only one dispensation – the dispensation of grace! The currently emphasized keynote is the secret, any moment rapture (a word not found in scripture) by means of which millions of Christians will suddenly vanish and escape the great seven year tribulation that will follow. Then they will return triumphantly with the Lord and reign with him one thousand years – The Millennium. Many are unaware that "post" and "a" millennial views have dominated at other times in church history.

Hal Lindsey and others have made this a popular and profitable view. (I have decided not to deal with the recent *Left Behind* series of barn burners.) Lindsey's *The Late Great Planet Earth* that appeared in 1970, maintains that the establishment of the nation of Israel in 1948 was THE big sign of Christ's return. Lindsey used Mark 13:30 to conclude that in one generation the end would come – i.e., 1988. In some circles the panic began and a great host have been panicked ever since. The date, of course, was wrong. Date setters are ubiquitous, even though Mark 13 is as plain as day, as plain as day three times: *But about that day or hour no one knows; you do not know when the time will come; you do not know when the master of the house will come.* If this were a power-point presentation, I would add a drum roll.

Jesus is right! No one knows the date for the end of the age. Hal Lindsey missed it but lived with the embarrassment all the way to the bank.

Scripture bending may have reached its zenith in one author's postulation that when Jesus says *"about that day or hour no one knows"* that does not mean we cannot know the month or year! So he wrote a book, *88 Reasons Why the Rapture Will Be in 1988,* and sold two million copies. Edgar Whisenant even dated the beginning of World War III: October 3, 1988.

"The last times are upon us." That line was written by Ignatius of Antioch during the early second century. Martin Luther wrote hopefully: "We have reached the time of the white (pale) horse of the Apocalypse. This world will not last any more, if God will, than another hundred years."[5]   One southern California minister published a book in 1978 with a line declaring that "the Lord is coming for his church before the end of 1981." Ten years later he declared, "Date setting is wrong, and I was guilty of coming close to that."[6] Date setting is not only wrong, it is impossible because we don't really know what time it is now! The Gregorian Calendar, the Common Calendar, is not the only game in town. In New York's Chinatown, the year 2000 was actually 4698. For our Jewish friends, it was 5760. Most scholars tell us that, according to our present calendar, Jesus was probably born about 6 B.C. The new millennium sneaked up on most of us before we had a chance to go into hyper.

Instead of giving his disciples the date for the end of the world, Jesus gives instruction for living in the light of not knowing when the end will come. The key words from

Mark 13 are: *"Keep alert! Keep awake! Watch!"* On May 19, 1780, in Hartford, Connecticut, a meeting of state legislators was plunged into darkness due to a sudden eclipse. Many believed it was the end of the world; some moved to adjourn. Colonel Davenport is reported to have said, "Mr. Speaker, if it is not the end of the world, I should choose to be found doing my duty. I move you, sir, that candles be brought."[7] Biblically, he was right on target. The parable Jesus tells in Mark 13:32-37 is the mountain top of the chapter from which we are to view everything else. The parable is unique to Mark and it is the only time the word *watch* appears in his gospel. In the middle of questions about the end of the world and dates, Jesus tells a story.

The story Jesus tells is about a landowner who goes away on a journey, puts his slaves in charge, *each with his work* (direct quote from the text), and commands the doorkeeper to be on watch. No one knows when he will return. What is important, Jesus says, is that when the master returns he not find his servants asleep on the job! His story (and the chapter) ends with the admonition: *"And what I say to you I say to all: Keep awake!"* The point of Mark 13 is vigilance, not calculation. The problem with the Doom Boom and so much of the current end of the world writing is that it is so pessimistic. Jesus was not a pessimist. He brought glory, wonder, salvation, healing, and joy into all of life. His followers are to do the same. My suggestion during these dark times is: "Bring in the candles and let's have light everywhere so that we can be found doing our duty, our work in the world."

The other admonition that we ought to take seriously, and post where we can see it every day, is Jesus' word to us in Mark 13:7: *"Do not be alarmed."* We ought not be caught up in end-time hysteria; we ought to be caught up in confident daily living. The focus of our lives ought not be on when things will wrap up but on the tasks assigned to us that have not been completed. We are not to be frantic but faithful. We are not to be those who know when time will end but those who know what to do with the time we have now.

Back in 1959, my wife and I went to see the movie *On the Beach.* It was the most "religious" movie experience I have ever had. The setting of the movie is Australia where people are waiting for a nuclear war's radiation to reach them. They are the last people on earth and the deadly clouds are moving their way. The closing scene of the movie depicts a stretch of beach with the waves gently lapping the sand. A piece of paper blows across the sand in a world where all humanity is gone. The movie ended and the capacity audience departed in eerie silence. Is this the way the world will end? Is this what Jesus is talking about? Did you note his words: *"This is but the beginning of the birthpangs"?* William Barclay translates: *"These things are the beginning of the birth-pangs of the new age."*

Mark 13 and the book of Revelation are not about the end, they are about a new beginning. From Revelation 21: *Then I saw a new heaven and a new earth....And I saw the holy city, the new Jerusalem, coming down out of heaven from God....Death will be no more; mourning and crying and pain will be no more, for the first things have passed away.* I read two lines in a book and added a line of my own. The author writes: "The message of Genesis is not to trace human history back to Adam. The message of Genesis is to trace human history back to God."[8] I wrote in the margin: And the purpose of Revelation is to trace the future of human history to God.

Mark 13, Revelation, and countless other scriptures assert that history is going somewhere. Apocalyptic passages assure us that one day our prayer will be answered: *Thy kingdom come, thy will be done on earth as it is in heaven.* Some day there will be the triumph of justice, goodness, righteousness, truth, hope, mercy, grace, and love. When? I don't know. Maybe tomorrow, or next week, or two hundred years from now. Who knows? What I do know is how we are to live and what we are to be doing.

> *Now concerning the times and the seasons, brothers and sisters, you do not need to have anything written to you. For you yourselves know very well that the day of the Lord will come like a thief in the night....So then let us not fall asleep as others do, but let us keep awake and be sober; for those who sleep at night, and those who are drunk get drunk at night. But since we belong to the day, let us be sober, and put on the breastplate of faith and love, and for a helmet the hope of salvation....Therefore encourage one another and build up each other, as indeed you are doing.* (I Thessalonians 5:1-2, 6-8, 11).

Reflections

I grew up in a church where Sunday night sermons and Wednesday night Bible studies often included an array of impressive charts. The material always included the list of "Dispensations" (after John Nelson Darby and the Scofield Bible), anti-Christ possibilities, and probable dates for end-time events. It was the presentation of Pre-Millennial Dispensational Theology. I was taught this was the clear – and only – teaching of scripture. It was only much later that I learned this was a relatively recent development and that there were other ways to read the scriptures.

The abundance of end-time materials today is staggering. One person keyed in the book of Revelation on the internet and was offered a choice of 2,666,896 web sites![9] What I find more interesting (and what I have checked out) is what is called "The Rapture Index." This site lets us know how close we are to the Rapture based on its author's analysis of what is being "fulfilled" in his prophesy index. End of the world predictions have always been with us and up until this present moment have all been mistaken. This observation: "Daniel 9 is probably the most difficult passage of the Old Testament to translate, let alone interpret, but it forms the basis for much of the current conservative understanding endtime chronology."[10]

Confidence in the final consummation of the ages is one thing. A preoccupation with signs, predictions, and endtime thinking is another. I think I'll just let God take care of wrapping things up.

[1]Marva J. Dawn, *Joy in Our Weakness,* revised edition (Grand Rapids, William B. Eerdmans Publishing Company, 2002), 193.

[2]Richard Kyle, *The Last Days Are Here Again* (Grand Rapids, Baker Books, 1998), 10-11.

[3]Richard Kyle, *The Last Days Are Here Again,* 99.

[4]Ibid. 175.

[5]Ibid. 55.

[6]Ibid. 120.

[7]Barbara Brown Taylor, *Gospel Medicine* (Boston, Cowley Publications, 1995), 136.

[8]R. Kirby Godsey, *When We Talk About God* (Macon, Smyth & Helwys, 1996), 81.

[9]Richard Holloway, *Revelations* (Edinburg, Canongate, 2005), 382.

[10]Jim Willis and Barbara Willis, *Armageddon: The End of the World A to Z* (New York, Fall River Press, 2006), 135.

Chapter 14: The Biggest Surprise About Judgment Day

MODERN OBSERVATIONS:

Imagine your having no need at all to judge anybody. Imagine your having no desire to decide whether someone is a good or bad person. Imagine your being completely free from the feeling that you have to make up your mind about the morality of someone's behavior. Imagine you could say: "I am judging no one!" Imagine – Wouldn't that be true inner freedom? The desert fathers from the fourth century said: "Judgment of others is a heavy burden."[1]

Let every tub stand upon its own bottom. John Bunyan, *The Pilgrim's Progress.*

THE BIBLICAL TEXT: Romans 14:10-12:

> *Why do you pass judgment on your brother or sister? Or you, why do you despise your brother or sister? For we will all stand before the judgment seat of God. For as it is written, "As I live, says the Lord, every knee shall bow to me, and every tongue shall give praise to God." So then, each of us will be accountable to God.*

The specific matters involved in the text from Romans 14 may seem remote but the questions Paul asks are as relevant as ever: *Why do you pass judgment on your brother or sister? Or you, why do you despise your brother or sister?* We need to note the context in which Paul wrote so that we can better discuss the issue in our context. The questions are addressed to believers living in Rome. Both the city and the church were cosmopolitan; backgrounds and approaches to life and the Christian faith differed. Not everybody saw things with a single eye.

The major points of contention were the eating of meat and the observance of special days. Almost all meat sold on the open market had been offered as a sacrifice to some pagan deity. Some felt no Christian could possibly eat it; others felt it really didn't matter since pagan gods were not gods at all. Those who observed special days were probably those who insisted the Jewish Sabbath should be strictly kept as well as the Lord's Day (Sunday); others saw no such necessity. The problem was the stance of judgment, no doubt with phrases like: "If you are a real Christian you will....," "Everybody knows that....," "I can't understand how anyone could possibly...," "How could anyone think like that?" The harshness of judgment is revealed in the fact that it led those involved to despise one another.

Whenever Charlie Brown and Linus stand with their elbows propped on the wall, you know weighty matters are up for discussion. Linus speaks first: "I have a theological question. When you die and go to heaven, are you graded on a percentage or a curve?" Charlie Brown answers, "On a curve, naturally." "How can you be so sure?" asks Linus. Confidently Charlie Brown responds, "I'm always sure about things that are a matter of opinion." The larger question in our discussion needs to be asked: Is this a matter of opinion? For those of us in the community of faith, it is not. Biblically, there is a consistent and prominent answer to the question Linus asks. Paul addresses it in Romans 14 and for many it is the biggest surprise about judgment day.

We begin with what ought to be obvious: we are not the judges, we are the judged. *For we must all stand before the judgment seat of God.* God is the judge; no one has the right to assume the role God has reserved for himself. We are all persons under judgment. When Paul writes that *each of us will be accountable to God,* the word *accountable* is a bookkeeping term. God will examine the ledger of our lives. In writing to the Corinthians about the nature of the Lord's judgment, Paul uses the phrases *bring to light* and *disclose the purposes of the heart* (I Corinthians 4:5). Beyond "just the facts," judgment involves motives, desires, and intentions. *So it will be on the day when, according to my gospel, God will judge the secrets of human hearts through Christ Jesus* (Romans 2:16).[2] God reserves for himself that which only God is capable of doing. A fuller and more literal translation of what Paul writes is: *It is to God, then, that each of us will give an account of himself/herself.*[3] God is not going to pass out evaluation sheets for our assessments of others. After the resurrected Lord gives Peter his marching orders, Peter looks toward John and asks, *"Lord, what about him?"* Jesus' rather curt reply is: *"...what is that to you? Follow me!"* (John 21:21-22).

From somewhere I picked up this reminder: "I have a point of view. You have a point of view. Only God has view." From our limited points of view we can never see what God is able to see. The insights Jesus gives into the final judgment reveal that God never runs out of surprises. Many who have awarded themselves first prize will find their ribbons given to those they designated as life's losers (Matthew 19:30). Some of the sheep will be dismayed to find themselves reclassified as goats and some of the goats will be equally jolted to discover they are included in the flock (Matthew 25:31-46). God reserves to himself the role of judge and all the envelopes are sealed until he opens them.

Many commentators note that what should be emphasized is the certainty and not the severity of God's judgment. Somewhere I found this anecdote: A sales agent knocked on the front door of a home. When no one answered, he glanced in the front window and saw a young lad practicing the piano. Their eyes met, and the young pianist eagerly jumped up and answered the door. "Is your mother at home?" inquired the salesman. "Now, what do you think?" the boy came back. The young man at practice made the question irrelevant. Paul would say that God is always in and, while he may not keep popping in to see if we are practicing, ultimately there will be a final recital to see how we have done with the piece assigned to us. This is not bad news; it is incredibly good news. Who we are and what we do matters so much to God that he holds us accountable. Nothing helped motivation in school any more than a "yes" to the question "Will this be on the test?" This is not a "Oh, what difference does it make, nobody will take notice" life. The fact of judgment, the fact of accountability, imputes value to us and our lives. We matter. What we do matters.

This chapter could have been titled "The Two Biggest Surprises About Judgment Day" because of what we are about to discuss. Judgment day for the redeemed is not a rehashing of sins and failures; the message of forgiveness is the message of forgetting: *You will cast all our sins into the depths of the sea* (Micah 7:19); *I will be merciful toward their iniquities, and I will remember their sins no more* (Hebrews 8:12). A large and encouraging sidebar is, that when writing to believers, Paul views judgment day more like "awards day." Here are three different translations of I Corinthians 4:5: (1) *Then each one will receive commendation from God* (NRSV); *(2) And then to each one there shall come...praise from God;*[4] (3) *Everyone will receive from God what he deserves.*[5] This is the time for applause and smiling and laughter and congratulations. This text seems to imply that the Lord "will find cause for approval where another judge would find none."[6] This is the fulfillment of the repeated closing request in Psalm 90: *Establish the work of our hands for us – yes, establish the work of our hands.*[7] God keeps a record of our faithfulness; He keeps a permanent record of all that is good. Jesus said that even if all we can do is give a cup of water in his name, that would be remembered (Mark 9:41). Recorded. Recognized.

One person's nightmare was standing in line where credentials for heaven were being checked, finding himself behind Mother Teresa, and hearing the Lord say to her, "You really could have done a little more." If that were to become reality, I think I would just step out of the line. That is, of course, assuming I'm going to be compared with Mother Teresa. That is a nightmare and it isn't true. The biggest surprise about judgment day is that we will not be judged in relation to anyone else. Charlie Brown is wrong; none of that grading on a curve stuff where, because somebody makes 100% on the test, your score of 90% becomes a C-. The good news of this is expressed in the English proverb: "Everyone must row with the oars he has." Those dashing by us in speedboats will not become the standard by which God judges our efforts – sometimes noteworthy is just keeping our boat afloat! Don't compare yourself with the super-achievers and conclude you are a failure. This is the fatal miscalculation of the steward in the parable of the "talents"(Matthew 25:14-30). (We are really talking about the investment of money, not "talents.") Because he has only a single talent, he buries it and returns it to the Master of the house unused (un-invested). To the other two stewards who invest their five talents and two talents respectively, the Master has the identical commendation: *"Well done, good and faithful servant."* The unfaithful servant is condemned because he did not invest what he had, not because he didn't invest what he didn't have.

Paul does not hesitate to include some specific instruction about the investments in our lives:

> *Some judge one day to be better than another, while others judge all days alike.* *LET ALL BE FULLY CONVINCED IN THEIR OWN MINDS* (Emphasis mine). *Those who observe the day, observe it in honor of the Lord. Also those who eat, eat in honor of the Lord, since they give thanks to God; while those who abstain, abstain in honor of the Lord and give thanks to God* (Romans 14:5-6).

I have always found it intriguing that Paul never gives an opinion about which side is right. His instruction is that all of them make certain whatever they do is done by conviction and that they do not sit in judgment on those who do not live by the same conviction.

In *"A Man for All Seasons,"* a young Cambridge scholar, Richard Rich, comes to Sir Thomas More for some vocational guidance. More suggests, "Why not be a teacher?

You'd be a fine teacher. Perhaps even a great one." Rich is taken aback and retorts, "And If I was, who would know it?" More replies, "You, your pupils, your friends, God. Not a bad public, that....Not bad at all."[8] Not a bad public at all and the real public to keep in mind. I have always been amazed at how many spend an inordinate amount of time trying to please people who really don't care that much about them. You won't find a better check and balance system for your convictions than Sir Thomas More's public.

I have kept until last what I consider the most important fact about judgment day. According to numerous scriptures, the person of the judgment is to be Jesus Christ. The Father has assigned to him this responsibility. Frederick Buechner notes: "In other words, the one who judges us most finally will be the one who loves us most fully."[9] When you inquire as to how someone is doing, you often get the response, "Pretty well, all things considered." That is what the final judgment is about – the consideration of all things by the one who fully understands all things. The basic reason we cannot pass judgment is that we don't know all the things that need to be considered. All things will be considered by the one who has perfect view and perfect understanding.

The best summation of this subject I have found is in this modern paraphrase of a portion of Romans 14:10:

> *What's important in all this is that if you keep a holy day, keep it for God's sake; if you eat meat, eat it to the glory of God and thank God for prime rib; if you're a vegetarian, eat vegetables to the glory of God and thank God for broccoli. None of us are permitted to insist on*

our own way in these matters. It's God we are answerable to – all the way from life to death and everything in between – not each other....So where does that leave you when you criticize a brother? And where does that leave you when you condescend to a sister? I'd say it leaves you looking pretty silly – or worse. Eventually, we're all going to end up kneeling side by side in the place of judgment, facing God. Your critical and condescending ways aren't going to improve your position one bit....[10]

Reflections

I would like to tell you that I have always welcomed criticism (and judgment) because I have found it to be so constructive and helpful to me in my personal life and ministry. To coin a classic phrase: "It ain't so!" Not only in my own personal life (and the life of my family) and in the lives of other ministers I have known, most criticism and judgment have been the source of incredible pain and often much irreparable damage. But they are not going away and will be experienced by almost everyone in some form or another.

I do believe in evaluation and accountability. These are a part of life now and we have indications they will be a part of what we can expect when this life is over. I repeat, this means that who we are and what we do matters. It also means that I will give an account only for myself and will not be asked my opinion of others. There is this classic bit: A counselor answered the phone and an anxious voice said, "We've got marriage problems. Can I send my wife to see you?" Accountability Day will be my "opportunity" to look at myself and no one else. The blame game will be over.

My great comforting thought is that I am only responsible for what I have been given. Supposedly it was Einstein who said, "Just because a fish can't climb a tree doesn't mean it's stupid." A fish is not meant to climb a tree – we know that. Each of us has unique gifts that enable us to do certain things; we are not equipped to do all things. I have finally learned to say, "That's okay."

One evaluation, one judgment is all that really matters. I need to remember that.

[1]Henri J. Nouwen, *The Mystery and the Passion* (Minneapolis, Fortress Press, 1992), 46.

[2]*Revised English Bible* (Oxford University Press, 1989).

[3]*The New Jerusalem Bible* (New York, Doubleday, 1985).

[4]Kenneth S. Wuest, *The New Testament: An Expanded Translation* (Grand Rapids, William B. Eerdmans Publishing Company, 1961).

[5]*Good News Bible* (New York, American Bible Society, 1976).

[6]F. F. Bruce, *I & II Corinthians: The New Century Bible Commentary* (Grand Rapids, William B. Eerdmans Publishing Company, 1983), 46.

[7]*New International Version* (International Bible Society, 1973).

[8]Quoted in Kelly Monroe, *Finding God at Harvard* (Grand Rapids, Zondervan Publishing Company, 1996), 306.

[9]Frederick Buechner, *Wishful Thinking* (New York, Harper & Row, 1973), 48.

[10]Eugene Peterson, *The Message* (Colorado Springs, Navpress, 2002).

Chapter 15: The Father's House: A Promise, Not a Blueprint

MODERN OBSERVATIONS:

Theorists of religious language remind us that we have not otherworldly or supernatural language by which to portray the transcendent; we have only human language and experience.[1]

The most obvious and striking feature of Jesus' view of life after death and the final state of our existence is that it is a *kingdom*. It is therefore social in nature. Jesus did not talk about some mystical flight of the alone to the alone. Although...finding the kingdom may involve such experiences, Jesus saw our final state as essentially a fellowship.[2]

A continual looking forward to the eternal world is not a form of escapism or wishful thinking, but one of the things a Christian is meant to do. It does not mean that we are to leave the present world as it is. If you read history, you will find that the Christians who did the most for the present world were just those who thought most of the next. C. S. Lewis.

THE BIBLICAL TEXT: John 14:1-3:

> "Do not let your hearts be troubled. Trust in God; trust also in me. In my Father's house are many rooms; if it were not so, I would have told you. I go to prepare a place for you. And if I go and prepare a place for you, I will come back and take you to be with me that you also may be where I am.[3]

Verb tenses are often crucial for the proper understanding of a text; this passage is a case in point. *"Stop being troubled"* is Jesus' admonition to his disciples who hear this none too soon. Much is troubling them as a result of Jesus' recent announcements: one of them will betray him (13:10-11, 18, 21), another will deny him three times (13:38), and he is going where none of them can follow (13:33, 36). What most troubles his followers is that Jesus keeps talking about dying. Behind every other troubling thing in life lurks this ultimate, universal, and inevitable chunk of trouble.

It is stated in various ways with varying degrees of gravity. H. L. Mencken provides one of the harsher renderings:

> *What the meaning of human life may be I don't know. I am inclined to suspect that it has none. All I know about it is that to me at least it is very amusing while it lasts....When I die, I shall be content to vanish into nothingness. No show, however good, could conceivable be good forever.*[4]

Comments in a lighter vain were overheard and reported a few years ago in the Metropolitan Diary of *The New York times:*

> *An elderly woman was passing through the cosmetics department of Bloomingdale's when a saleswoman carrying a tray of "free gift with purchase" products asked if there was anything she would like to buy. "I don't need anything at the moment," she answered. The saleswoman offered, "That's no problem. Our products have a shelf life of two years." The woman smiled and said, "The difficulty is, I'm not sure of my shelf life."*

Woody Allen summed it up for many when asked if he believed in the afterlife: "Yes, but I'm afraid no one will tell me where it's being held." I believe that is exactly what someone did.

I believe Jesus is the only one who ever gave us an effective way to deal with our "terminal anxiety." The common approaches most frequently used in dealing with this basic fear involve busyness, distraction, or the Scarlett O'Hara method, "I'll think about that tomorrow." Many find it helpful to put a smiley face on the grim reaper in hopes that humor will alleviate some of the foreboding. (A funeral director was reported to have signed all his correspondence, "Eventually yours.") In confronting the big troubler in life, Jesus gives an alternative to busyness, distraction, postponement, or humor. His prescription: *"Trust in God; trust also in me."* The verb tenses in Jesus' invitation make it even more immediate: *"Be putting your trust in God. Also be putting your trust in me."*

When all is said and done (and there will be a time when all is finally said and all is finally done), no one can provide scientific proof for an afterlife. (Lazarus was not debriefed. In fact, there is not a single recorded word from this brother of Mary and Martha, a family very special to Jesus in his adult life.) Our confidence issues from our belief that God is trustworthy, Jesus is trustworthy. This is faith that the creator-covenant-making God revealed in Holy Scripture is the author and sustainer of life, of all that is or ever shall be, and he will not allow anything to remove us from his care (Romans 8:38-39). This is faith that Jesus is God's first installment in his resurrection plan for all of his children (I Corinthians 15:20). (The subject of resurrection will be explored further in Chapter 16.) We often forget that the only reason Christians gather in worship on Sunday morning is that 2,000 years ago a group of people began running around (notice how everyone runs in the gospel resurrection accounts) shouting, "He's alive! He's alive!" And nobody could shut them up. Religious persecution couldn't shut them up. Imperial edicts couldn't shut them up. Lion-filled arenas couldn't shut them up. They believed and kept bearing witness to the most fantastic claim ever made in the history of the world! Their testimony to us today is: "He did it! God did what Jesus said he would do. He raised him up! You really can trust God. You really can trust Jesus."

We are not talking about the immortality of the soul, which is not a biblical teaching, but resurrection, which is. Years ago, I found this intriguing argument:

> *When I urge people to chuck the immortality of the soul as a piece of anti-Gospel baggage, they worry. They tell me, "Look, this is 1997. What about 2097? If I don't have an immortal soul, and the Rapture doesn't happen in the meantime, where will I be then?" I tell them, "You look: what are you worried about? You were nothing in 1797, and it hasn't bothered you so far. Why should it bother you now? Can't God do the same trick the second time? Hasn't he promised to do exactly that?*[5]

Yes, he has. According to Jesus, it will be resurrection in the Father's house.

The primary notation is that it is the Father's house. This is the house of the God and Father we have come to know in Jesus Christ. This is the God of Abraham, Sarah,

Isaac, Rebecca, Jacob, Joseph, Moses, Rahab, Gideon, Samson, David, Samuel (see Hebrews 11) and Isaiah. This is the God who has proved himself so trustworthy and faithful that he is called rock, fortress, deliverer, and the great shepherd who is unconditionally committed to the care of his sheep. Jesus doesn't go into any details about the next life. *"In my Father's house"* is all he deemed necessary to quell the anxious hearts of his disciples.

C. S. Lewis has provided the classic approach to interpreting biblical metaphors concerning the next life:

> *All the scriptural imagery (harps, crowns, gold, etc.) is, of course, a merely symbolical attempt to express the inexpressible. Musical instruments are mentioned because for many people (not all) music is the thing known in the present life which most strongly suggests ecstasy and infinity. Crowns are mentioned to suggest the fact that those who are united with God in eternity share His spendour and power and joy. Gold is mentioned to suggest the timelessness of Heaven (gold does not rust) and the preciousness of it. People who take these symbols literally might as well think that when Christ told us to be like doves, He meant that we were to lay eggs.*[6]

Jesus assures us that in the Father's house *are many rooms.* The King James Version translates the Greek word *monai* as *mansions.* Tyndale took this term directly from the Latin *mansions* which means an "abode, dwelling place, habitation, rest camp, or way station," as does the Greek *monai.* The emphasis in the original word itself was on a place to stay rather than on the impressiveness of the place.[7] This is much better news than the assurance of a palatial residence. The biblical designation means that none who arrive at the Father's house will see a "No Vacancy" sign hanging out in front. Another way to translate John 14:2 is: *In my Father's house there is room for all."* More specifically, Jesus says, "I've made an advance reservation for you. When you get to the front desk and they ask for your confirmation number, just give them my name. Tell them I reserved a place for you."

There will not only be room for all but there will be room for a whole lot more. Paul sums up heavenly expectations in I Corinthians 2:9: *...as it is written: "No eye has seen, no ear has heard, no mind has conceived what God has prepared for those who love him."* A more modern writer has said that the best way a Christian can prepare for death is to develop a healthy capacity for surprise.[8] I like to use this analogy: If you ask as you are checking into the Father's house, "Does my room have a view?" I am certain the answer will be, "Oh, yes!" If you inquire further, "What will I be able to see?" I think the reply will be, "Everything!"

Jesus emphasizes that he will be with his disciples in the Father's house: *"...that you may also be where I am."* Jesus describes heaven in terms of relationships. The next life means "a full personal life with powers of communication of person with person."[9] When someone asks, "Will we recognize one another in the next life?" my response is always the same: "If we didn't, it wouldn't be heaven." If the importance of relationships is expressed in the great commandment to love God with all our heart, mind, soul, and strength and our neighbor as ourselves, certainly the next life will continue, deeper, and expand those relationships.

We don't have to worry about how we'll get to the Father's house: transportation will be furnished. *"And if I go and prepare a place for you, I will come back and take you to be with me...."* (When someone worries excessively about how they will get located in the next life, I ask them what arrangements they made to get here in the first place.) Just as the beginning of everything was in God's hands, so is the ending. We believe in the One who is the Alpha and Omega, the beginning and the end (Revelation 21:6). We believe in the consummation of history. We believe that there is purpose, completion, and final destination to everything in life. We are told that Abraham was looking for a city whose architect and builder is God (Hebrews 11:10). We believe he will find it. And so will we.

In November 1996 the funeral service for Joseph Cardinal Bernardin was held in Chicago. John Buchanan, Senior Minister of the Fourth Avenue Presbyterian Church attended the service (as did the Vice-President of the United States, the Governor, and the Mayor) and provided these observations:

> *The homily was delivered by Monsignor Father Kenneth Velo, Cardinal Bernardin's longtime friend and assistant. It was a spirited and eloquent and sometimes very funny and altogether human address. He concluded with a touchingly personal word – "Cardinal, eminence. You're home. You're home." And then the most remarkable liturgical act I have ever witnessed and participated in occurred. It wasn't listed in the program. I don't think anybody – even with the exquisite and detailed planning that obviously had taken place – anticipated it. Father Velo sat down. There was a moment of empty silence. And then, someone started to*

*applaud. Instantly, everybody joined. AND then
everybody stood. The people in the pews first, and at last,
the hierarchy, the bishops and archbishops and cardinals
and papal nuncios – who, because they were seated behind
the high altar were actually facing the congregation and
could see it themselves. This wasn't in the liturgical
program. It began appropriately in the back, and finally
they, too, stood to engage in this unscheduled and
remarkable liturgical ovation.*[10]

J. B. Phillips has suggested it would be more
appropriate to refer to those whose physical body had died
as the "arrived" rather than as the "departed." I agree.
Arrived where? Why, in the Father's house, of course.

Reflections

My favorite quote about the next life has always
been this one from C. S. Lewis: "Guesses, of course,
guesses. If they are not true, something better will be." I
believe that just about sums it up because of what Paul
writes in II Corinthians 4:17: *For this slight momentary
affliction is preparing for us an eternal weight of glory beyond
all measure....*Literally, the Greek reads *the excessively to
excess.* That is the best description of the Father's house I
have ever read: the excessively to excess. Paul was at a loss
for words to describe what the life hereafter would be like.
So are we. It is beyond our powers of description. But I do
always say this: I guarantee that you won't be disappointed!

[1]Wayne Martindale, *Journey To the Celestial City* (Chicago, Moody Press, 1995), 23.

[2]Morton T. Kelsey, *Afterlife* (New York, Crossroad Publishing Company, 1982), 162.

[3]*New International Version.*

[4]Quoted in John Sutherland Bonnell, *I Believe in Immortality* (Nashville, Abingdon Press, 1959), 12.

[5]Robert Farrar Capon, *The Foolishness of Preaching* (Grand Rapids, William B. Eerdmans Publishing Company, 1998), 25.

[6]Quoted in Peter Kreef, *The Shadow-lands of C.S. Lewis* (San Francisco, Ignatius Press, 1994), 69-70.

[7]*The Broadman Bible Commentary*, Volume 9 (Nashville, Broadman Press, 1970), 333.

[8]John Shea in Andrew Greeley, *Death and Beyond* (Chicago, The Thomas More Press, 1976), 124.

[9]John Sutherland Bonnell, *I Believe in Immortality*, 60.

[10]*Homiletics*, Volume 9, Number 3, July-September 1997, 17.

Chapter 16: Faith's Equation: Christianity Minus Resurrection Equals Nothing

MODERN OBSERVATIONS:

Jesus did not return to his disciples as a ball of fire or an inner voice, but as a resurrected body which could be handled and touched and which consumed fish....There is little doubt that these appearances of Jesus were the cornerstone of the faith of early Christianity. They convinced the disciples that Jesus had conquered death, and with this conviction they were able to go forth and outlive, out-think, and out-die the ancient world.[1]

The Pauline letters predate the Gospels and, therefore, may offer the earliest witness to the resurrection. Of all the Pauline writings, I Corinthians 15 contains the most developed presentation of the resurrection message....Most scholars agree that the creedal recitation in I Corinthians 15:1-11 is no doubt the earliest testimony to the resurrection.[2]

Accounts of the discovery of the empty tomb sound breathless and fragmentary. The women were "afraid and filled with joy," says Matthew; "trembling and bewildered," says Mark. Jesus makes no dramatic, well-orchestrated entrance to quell all doubts; the early reports seem wispy, mysterious, confused. Surely conspirators could have done a neater job of depicting what they would later claim to be the hinge event of history. In short, the Gospels do not present the resurrection of Jesus in the manner of apologetics, with arguments arranged to prove each main point, but rather as a shocking intrusion that no one was expecting, least of all Jesus' timorous disciples.[3]

THE BIBLICAL TEXT: I Corinthians 15:12-26:

Now if Christ is proclaimed as raised from the dead, how can some of you say there is no resurrection of the dead? If there is no resurrection of the dead, then Christ has not been raised; and if Christ has not been raised, then our proclamation has been in vain and your faith has been in vain. We are even found to be misrepresenting God, because we testified of God that he raised Christ – whom he did not raise if it is true that the dead are not raised. For if the dead are not raised, then Christ has not been raised. If Christ has not been raised, your faith is futile and you are still in your sins. Then those also who have died in Christ have perished. If for this life only we have hoped in Christ, we are of all people to be pitied.

But in fact Christ has been raised from the dead, the first fruits of those who have died. For since death came through a human being, the resurrection of the dead has also come through a human being; for as all die in Adam, so all will be made alive in Christ. But each in his own order: Christ the first fruits, then at his coming those who belong to Christ. Then comes the end, when he hands over the kingdom to God the Father, after he has destroyed every ruler and every authority and power. For he must reign until he has put all his enemies under his feet. The last enemy to be destroyed is death.

Paul begins this portion of his letter (actually letters) to the Corinthians with the rejoinder: *I want to remind you of the gospel I preached to you, which you received and on which you have taken your stand.*[4]   All too often it is assumed that those within the church understand what is meant by the preaching of the gospel; Paul didn't make this assumption even with the first century converts at Corinth who had heard it personally from him. What is the *gospel* (literally the *good news)* that Paul had delivered and is so concerned

171

about preserving? On what have these first Christians taken their stand? Is the good news about a model teacher who left us a rich heritage of instruction like the Sermon on the Mount? Is the good news about a person who modeled for us what it means to live as a sensitive and caring human being? Is the good news about one who provides a source of inspiration and courage for meeting the challenges of today? My answer is: partly, yes, but primarily no, no. no.

Paul's summation of the gospel underscores that which genuinely makes it good news: *For I handed to you as of first importance what I in turn had received: that Christ died for our sins in accordance with the scriptures, and that he was buried, and that he was raised on the third day in accordance with the scriptures* (I Corinthians 15:3-4). What is of first importance is so important that without it the gospel is emptied entirely of its content. Mathematically speaking, faith's equation is: Christianity minus resurrection equals nothing. No sentence of Paul's is more dogmatic than his unyielding position that *if Christ has not been raised, then our proclamation has been in vain and your faith has been in vain.* The word we translate *vain* must have been chosen with great care: it means null, void, empty, worthless.

Here is a case where we put all our eggs into one basket; the early church put all its eggs in the same basket. This Easter basket is the bedrock of the Christian faith.

> *"This overturns our understanding of Christian beginnings. The beginning is not where many think it is. It is not the birth of Jesus. It is not the cross of Jesus. It is the resurrection of Jesus....For the first disciples the Gospel without the resurrection was not merely a Gospel without*

its final chapter, it was no Gospel at all.[5]

As dramatic and life-changing as Jesus' teaching and healing ministry must have been, after the crucifixion Peter announces, "I'm going fishing" and six of the other disciples join him in getting back to business as usual (John 21:2-3). The next morning, a figure on shore gives instruction that puts so many fish into their empty net that all seven of them can't pull it in. Ironically, this episode brings their fishing careers to an end.

It should be remembered that the gospels were written backward. First, the disciples confronted the risen Christ. Then they remembered his passion and crucifixion (and all he had tried to teach them about it). Then they collected his teachings and stories about his healing ministry. Then they reached back into their distant memories to the story of Jesus' birth. Christmas was one of the last festivals of the church to be celebrated; Easter was the first. Without the Easter celebration there would have been no others.[6] While Paul begins this Corinthian correspondence with *the message about the cross as the power of God* (1:18) and his decision *to know nothing among you except Jesus Christ, and him crucified* (2:2), this message is proclaimed in the light of the resurrection. Without the resurrection the cross would have no meaning and no power. The issue is not whether Jesus died. A part of the early confession of faith was *he was buried*. The question is: was this the end?

Paul almost shouts: "It wasn't the end! He was raised from the dead on the third day and he appeared to a great host of persons!" (Paul indicates this company in 15:5-

8: Peter, the twelve, five-hundred plus, James, all the apostles, and finally to "one untimely born.") The designation for the first followers of Christ was "witnesses of the resurrection." These are witnesses who never believed they would have anything to tell. No one expected resurrection: none of Jesus' disciples, none of his friends, none of his family. You do not find any of the disciples on Saturday eagerly anticipating some reversal of Good Friday. They were not waiting at all. They were either hiding behind locked doors for fear they might share his fate or they were getting out of town like the two on the Emmaus Road. The resurrection was totally unexpected. It was a complete surprise. In this vivid translation, Luke gives the reaction of the disciples to the women's story that Jesus has been raised: *Now the women, Mary Magdalene and Joanna and Mary, James's mother, and others with them, kept telling the same story to the apostles. But the words seemed humbug to them, and they did not believe.*[7] Of course, who would believe it? It is unbelievable! On top of everything, the first reports of Jesus' resurrection come from women whose testimony in that day was not formally admitted as public evidence. Some conjecture this is the reason, that in I Corinthians 15, they are omitted and the witnesses mentioned are men.

To make matters worse, the reports of the witnesses are confusing and impossible to arrange in logical order. This is not damaging to their testimonies, but verifying:

> *Indeed, the very discrepancies read, if anything, much more like eye-witness reports of the same confused, swift and frightening events than like an attempt, long afterwards, to construct a piece of fiction out of*

theological motivations.[8]

Most scholars have concluded that the original ending of the Gospel of Mark is verse eight of chapter sixteen. It is exactly what you would expect from such an unexpected event. The verse even ends in the middle of a sentence: *And going out (the women) ran from the tomb for they were beside themselves and shaking. No one said anything; for they were afraid for....*[9] These first witnesses had the appropriate first response: unbelief, shaking, wonder, fear. If this were true, it spoke to the most important question life offers, to the basic fear underlying all other fears, to the dread of all dreads. This is not a "religious" question. It surfaces frequently and often in unexpected places like a cartoon in the *New Yorker* magazine. An elderly man and an elderly woman are seated in rocking chairs on a porch. The man's words are captioned underneath: "No, I don't want to live forever, but I....sure don't want to be dead forever either."[10]

In the cemetery of an Episcopal church in rural Louisiana, in accordance with the woman's instructions, only one word is carved on her tombstone: "Waiting."[11] This is a word of hope and a word of promise. The celebration of Easter is not only about what God did for his Son, but what he will do for all of his children. The resurrection of Jesus is simply the first installment of God's great resurrection plan. Every time Paul speaks about Jesus' resurrection, he uses the same Greek verb tense (perfect tense of the passive voice), *has been raised to live (and is still alive).*[12] It was an act of God, a creative act of God. That is why many call Sunday the eighth day, the day of God's new creation in Christ Jesus. Christians do not believe in immortality of the soul, we believe in resurrection. We do not deny that death is real; we deny that it is final. We do not believe that resurrection is "natural." It is a sheer gift from God. Just as he gave us life in the beginning, so we believe he will give us new life.

I don't think anyone has captured this idea any better than Winston Churchill in making plans for his funeral. After the benediction, he directed that a trumpeter, high up in the Whispering Gallery of St. Paul's, would sound the Last Post (Taps). He then instructed that the trumpeter would sound Reveille. Six thousand people heard this Christian witness to Paul's prophecy: *The last enemy to be destroyed is death.* This will happen as the spiritual says, "in that great getting up morning." I believe in that great getting up morning because I believe these words: "the Resurrection of Christ means that God will always have the last word."

> If we believe in the loving God about whom Jesus preached, then we should have no trouble believing in the conquest of death, because God's love is stronger than death....Jesus lives and we will, too, because God does not abandon the ones he loves. And that is the bottom line of all bottom lines.[13]

This is the bottom line in the journey (struggle) from fear to faith. One day the promise of I John 4:18 will be brought to full fruition: *Perfect love banishes fear.*[14]

Reflections

I cannot imagine a funeral service that does not begin with the reading of John 11:25-26: *I am the resurrection and the life. Those who believe in me, even though they die, will live, and everyone who lives and believes in me will never die.* I have always wanted to make this a responsive reading by adding the last half of verse 26, *Do you believe this?*, and having the congregation respond as Mary did, *Yes, we believe! Amen!* What other words do we want to hear or need to hear at such a time?

"N. T. Wright contends that only three interlocking things can give us confidence that Jesus is risen – the empty tomb, the multiple apparitions, and the seismic change in the followers of Jesus."[15] J. S Whale puts it like this: "We cannot begin to know how it happened (the resurrection). The Gospels cannot explain the Resurrection; it is the Resurrection which alone explains the Gospels."[16]

I join with others who contend that if you were making up a story you would never make it up the way the gospel writers do when telling about the resurrection. The variations in the Easter stories are exactly what you would expect from eye witnesses to such a dramatic event. There is no attempt to meld the accounts into one consistent story. That's what you do if you were making it up. It was full of too much wonder and mystery for that. It still is.

[1]Morton Kelsey, *Afterlife* (New York, Crossroad Publishing Company, 1982), 148.

[2]David Buttrick, *The Mystery and the Passion* (Minneapolis, Fortress Press, 1992), 54-55.

[3]Philip Yancey, *The Jesus I Never Knew* (Grand Rapids, Zondervan Publishing House, 1995), 213.

[4]*New International Version.*

[5]Canterbury Cathedral Easter Sermon, 1996, quoted in *The Anglican Digest.*

[6]Adapted from Carl Rife in *Homiletics,* Volume 7, Number 4, October-December, 1995, 54.

[7]David Buttrick, *The Mystery and the Passion,* 75.

[8]Tom Wright, *The Original Jesus* (Grand Rapids, William B. Eerdmans Publishing Company, 1996), 99.

[9]David Buttrick, *The Mystery and the Passion,* 66.

[10]*New Yorker,* December 8, 1988, 75.

[11]Philip Yancey, *The Jesus I Never Knew,* 275.

[12]Robert G. Bratcher, *A Translator's Guide to Paul's First Letter to the Corinthians* (New York, United Bible Societies, 1982), 145.

[13]Andrew Greeley, *The Bottom Line Catechism* (Chicago, The Thomas More Press, 1982), 95-96.

[14]William Barclay, *The New Testament* (Louisville, Westminster John Knox, 1999).

[15]Gary Willis, *What Jesus Meant,* 124.

[16]J. S. Whale, *Christian Doctrine* (Cambridge, The University Press, 1966), 73.

"From Fear to Faith in Eternal Matters"

Points to Ponder

From the earliest New Testament times, believers have felt that the end was near.

Instead of giving his disciples the date for the end of the world, Jesus gives instructions for living in the light of not knowing when the end will come.

Mark 13 and the book of Revelation are not about the end, they are about a new beginning.

We are not the judges, we are the judged.

I have a point of view. You have a point of view. Only God has view.

God keeps a record of faithfulness; He keeps a permanent record of all that is good.

Paul's instruction in Romans 14 is we make certain that whatever we do is done by conviction and that we do not sit in judgment on those who do not live by the same conviction.

According to numerous scriptures, the person of the judgment is to be Jesus Christ.

Jesus is the only one who ever gave us an effective way to

deal with our "terminal anxiety."

Jesus doesn't go into any details about the next life. *"In my Father's house"* is all he deemed necessary to quell the anxious hearts of his disciples.

We don't have to worry about how we'll get to the Father's house; transportation will be provided.

No sentence of Paul's is more dogmatic that this unyielding position: *if Christ has not been raised, then our proclamation has been in vain and your faith has been in vain.*

Without the resurrection the cross would have no meaning and no power.

The response of the first witnesses to the resurrection is exactly what you would expect from such an unexpected event.

Hope's new mathematics: our faith in the resurrection equals everything.

Bibliography of Quoted Sources

Andrew, John. *Nothing Cheap and Much That is Cheerful.* Grand Rapids: Zondervan Publishing House, 1997.

Arterburn, Stephen. *The God of Second Chances.* Nashville: Thomas Nelson Publishers, 2002.

Austin, Thomas David. *Faith Journey of a Pilgrim.* Macon: Smyth & Helwys, 2000.

Barclay, William. *The Letters of James and Peter.* Philadelphia: Westminster Press, 1960.

_____. *Testament of Faith.* London: Mowbrays, 1975.

_____. *The New Testament.* Louisville: Westminster John Knox, 1999.

Baur, Francis. *Life in Abundance.* New York: Paulist Press, 1983.

Bonnell, John Sutherland. *I Believe in Immortality.* Nashville: Abingdon Press, 1959.

Boyd, Gregory A. *God of the Possible.* Grand Rapids: Baker Books, 2000.

Bratcher, Robert G. *A Translator's Guide to Paul's First Letter to the Corinthians.* New York: United Bible Societies, 1982.

Broadman Bible Commentary, The, vol. 12. Nashville: Broadman Press, 1972.

Brokaw, Tom. *The Greatest Generation.* New York: Random House, 1998.

Bruce, F. F. *I & II Corinthians: The New Century Bible Commentary.* Grand Rapids: William B. Eerdmans Publishing Company, 1983.

Brueggemann, Walter. *Theology of the Old Testament.* Minneapolis: Fortress Press, 1997.

Buechner, Frederick. *Telling Secrets.* New York: HarperSanFrancisco, 1992.

_____. *Wishful Thinking.* New York: Harper & Row, 1973.

Buttrick, David. *Mystery and the Passion, The.* Minneapolis: Fortress Press, 1992.

_____. *Preaching the New and the Now.* Louisville: Westminster John Knox, 1998.

Buttrick, George Arthur. *God, Pain, and Evil.* Nashville: Abingdon Press, 1966.

Capon, Robert Farrar. *The Foolishness of Preaching.* Grand Rapids: William B. Eerdmans Publishing Company, 1998.

Carmody, John. *How to Handle Trouble.* New York: Fawcett Columbine, 1993.

Carter, Jimmy. *Living Faith.* New York: Times Books, 1996.

Chopra, Deepak. *How To Know God.* New York: Harmony Books, 2000.

Coles, Robert. *Harvard Diary.* New York: Crossroad Publishing, 1997.

Cox, James, ed. *Best Sermons 4.* New York: HarperSanFrancisco, 1991.

Crenshaw, James L. *Trembling at the Threshold of a Biblical Text.* Grand Rapids: William B. Eerdmans Publishing Company, 1994.

Davids, Peter. *New International Greek Testament Commentary, Commentary on James.* Grand Rapids: William B. Eerdmans Publishing Company, 1998.

Davies, Robertson. *The Merry Heart.* New York: Viking, 1996.

Dawn, Marva J. *Joy in Our Weakness,* revised edition. Grand Rapids: William B. Eerdmans Publishing Company, 2002.

deMello, Anthony. *Awareness.* New York: Image Books, 1992.

_____. *Taking Flight.* New York: Image Books, 1990.

Dyke, Dick Van. *Faith, Hope, and Hilarity.* Garden City: Doubleday and Company, 1970.

Evely, Louis. *That Man Is You.* New York: The Newman Press, 1966.

_____. *We Dare To Say Our Father.* New York: Herder and Herder, 1989.

Fosdick, Harry Emerson. *A Great Time To Be Alive.* New York: Harper & Brothers, 1944.

Frey, William. *The Dance of Hope.* Colorado Springs: Waterbrook Press, 2003.

Gibson, John A. *Job.* Philadelphia: Westminster Press, 1985.

Godsey, R. Kirby. *When We Talk About God.* Macon: Smyth & Helwys, 1996.

Goldstein, Niles Elliot. *God At the Edge.* New York: Bell Tower, 2000.

Gomes, Peter. *Strength for the Journey.* New York: HarperOne, 2003.

Graves, Mike. *The Sermon as Symphony.* Valley Forge: Judson Press, 1997.

Greeley, Andrew. *Death and Beyond.* Chicago: The Thomas More Press, 1970.

Holloway, Richard. *Revelations.* Edinburg: Canongate, 2005.

Interpreter's Bible, The New. Nashville: Abingdon Press, 1996.

Kaminer, Wendy. *I'm Dysfunctional, You're Dysfunctional.* Reading, Massachusetts: Addison-Wesley Publishing Company, 1992.

Kelsey, Morton. *Afterlife.* New York: Crossroad Publishing Company, 1982.

Kreef, Peter. *The God Who Loves You.* Ann Arbor: Servant Books, 1988.

_____. *The Shadow-lands of C.S. Lewis.* San Francisco: Ignatius Press, 1994.

Kugel, James L. *The Great Poems of the Bible.* New York: The Free Press, 1999.

Kushner, Harold S. *When Bad Things Happen To Good People.* New York: Shocken Books, 1981.

Kyle, Richard. *The Last Days Are Here Again.* Grand Rapids: Baker Books, 1998.

Lewis, C.S. *God in the Dock.* Grand Rapids: William B. Eerdman's Publishing Company, 1970.

Malone, Nancy. *Walking a Literary Labyrinth.* New York: Riverhead Books, 2003.

Martindale, Wayne. *Journey To the Celestial City.* Chicago: Moody Press, 1995.

McLaren, Brian and Compolo, Tony. *Adventures in Missing the Point.* Grand Rapids: Zondervan, 2006.

Merton, Thomas. *No Man Is An Island.* New York: Harcourt Brace Jovanovich, 1995.

Miller, Calvin. *Life Is Mostly Edges.* Nashville: Thomas Nelson, 2008.

Monroe, Kelly. *Finding God at Harvard.* Grand Rapids: Zondervan Publishing Company, 1996.

Norris, Kathleen. *The Cloister Walk.* New York: Riverhead Books, 1996.

Nouwen, Henri J. M. *Here and Now.* New York: Crossroad, 1994.

_____. *The Mystery and the Passion.* Minneapolis: Fortress Press, 1992.

Peterson, Eugene. *A Long Obedience in the Same Direction.*

Downers Grove, Il.: Inter-Varsity Press, 1980.

_____. *The Message*. Colorado Springs: Navipress, 2002.

Rohr, Richard. *The Naked Now*. New York: Crossroad Publishing Company, 2001.

Rolheiser, Ronald. *Against an Infinite Horizon*. New York: Crossroad Publishing Company, 1992.

Seitz, Christopher R. *Interpretation*. Louisville: John Knox Press, 1993.

Shibley, David. *Recapturing Your Dreams*. Green Forest, AR.: New Leaf Press, 1988.

Simmons, Philip. *Learning To Fall: The Blessings of an Imperfect Life*. New York: Bantam Books, 2002.

Smith, Martin. *The Word Is Very Near You*. Cambridge: Cowley Publications, 1989.

Stackhouse, John G., Jr. *Humble Apologetics*. Oxford: Oxford University Press, 2002.

Steindle-Rast, David. *Gratefulness, the Heart of Prayer*. New York: Paulist Press, 1984.

Stewart, James S. *The Strong Name*. New York: Charles Scribner's Sons, 1941.

Sweet, Leonard. *A Cup of Coffee at the Soul Café*. Nashville: Broadman & Holman Publishers, 1998.

_____. *Soul Tsunami*. Grand Rapids: Zondervan Publishing House, 1999.

Taylor, Barbara Brown. *Gospel Medicine*. Boston: Crowley Publications, 1995.

Taylor, David. *The Myth of Christianity*. Waco: Jarrell, 1986.

Weatherhead, Leslie D. *That Immortal Sea*. New York: Abingdon Press, 1953.

_____. *Time for God*. Nashville: Abingdon, 1967.

Whale, J. S. *Christian Doctrine*. Cambridge: The University Press, 1966.

Willard, Dallas. *The Divine Conspiracy*. New York: HarperSanFrancisco, 1998.

Willis, Jim and Willis, Barbara. *Armageddon: The End of the World A to Z*. New York: Fall River Press, 2006.

Wolpe, David J. *In Speech and In Silence*. New York: Henry Holt and Company, 1992.

Wright, Tom. *The Original Jesus*. Grand Rapids: William B.

Eerdman's Publishing Company, 1996.

Wuest, Kenneth. *The New Testament: An Expanded Translation.* Grand   Rapids:William B. Eerdmans Publishing Company, 1962.

Yancey, Philip. *Disappointment With God.* Grand Rapids: Zondervan Publishing House, 1998.

_____. *Jesus I Never Knew, The.* Grand Rapids: Zondervan Publishing House, 1995.

_____. *Reaching for the Invisible God.* Grand Rapids: Zondervan Publishing House, 2000.

_____. *Where Is God When It Hurts?* Grand Rapids: Zondervan Publishing House, 1990.

Yount, David. *Ten Thoughts To Take Into Eternity.* New York: Simon & Schuster, 1999.

Scripture Index

Scripture Index

About the Author

Ron Higdon has had over fifty years of pastoral experience. Presently, he is a certified church consultant and intentional interim specialist; he received his training and certification through the Center for Congregational Health in Winston-Salem, North Carolina. He has served churches in Kentucky, Virginia, North Carolina, Texas, and Georgia. In addition to his work as a church consultant, he personally leads study-groups on this book. He and his wife live in Prospect, Kentucky (a suburb of Louisville) and have two grown sons who live in Atlanta.

His email address is: rbooks5000@aol.com.

www.ingramcontent.com/pod-product-compliance
Lightning Source LLC
Chambersburg PA
CBHW031258090426
42742CB00007B/512